THE SUMMIT SEEKER: MEMOIRS OF A TRAIL RUNNING NOMAD

BY

VANESSA RUNS

Vanessa Runs

Book Design: Y42K Publication Services/y42k.com

First edition

ISBN: 1482502933
ISBN-13: 978-1482502930

Dedication

To Shacky, without whom none of my adventures would be possible.

Vanessa Runs

Table of Contents

Vanessa Runs

Foreword

by Gordon Ainsleigh

Many, many years ago, in one of my rare moments watching television, I was taking in Dick Cavett interviewing Truman Capote, who had made quite a stir with his rather thick books, most notably *In Cold Blood*, that dwelt on the intimate details of horrific crimes and horrific criminals. The conversation went something like this:

Cavett to Capote: "You always write books about these terrible crimes. Is that because, if you wrote a book about ordinary people, no one would want to read it because it just wouldn't be interesting?"

Capote: "Oh, no, not at all! Ordinary people have fascinating lives...absolutely fascinating...if you could ever get them to tell the truth. But they won't, of course. But when an horrendous crime has been committed, and everything has been investigated down to the smallest detail, and all the secrets are out, then people will tell the truth, and it makes a good book."

It's true: many ordinary people have fascinating lives, and, for a few years in my mid-twenties when I worked as a counselor, I occasionally got to experience the encompassing drama to which Truman Capote devoted his life: when people tell the deep hidden truths of their lives.

So what happens when a person who isn't ordinary—Vanessa, for instance—tells the truth about her life? Well, it's a bit of a wild ride, and a ride upon which you are about to embark in this book, a book by Vanessa, on Vanessa.

Some of what you experience will resonate deeply in your soul with some moments in your own life that stir within you until the day you die. You will feel that you and Vanessa are breathing the same air, feeling the same sun, facing the same emptiness, and exulting the same joy.

And then she will take you where you never imagined you could ever go. She allows us to live more than our one, too small life. She reminds me that no one in my life to whom I was deeply attached ever died until my grandmother—who played mom while my mother was out earning a living, playing dad—died at the age of 90. Vanessa's mother died when she was nine. We get to live that death, and the functional death of her father that followed, with Vanessa, and it fills in the empty places in our experience as human beings.

Vanessa takes us where we have never gone, and where we have always been. We are shocked by how different her life is from ours, and then, at other times, how much the same. The path she takes us on is a roller coaster between life-ways and events that we could never have imagined, and then on to events as common to us all as remarking on our digestive processes during passage down wildland trails at five to 10 miles per hour.

When I first met Vanessa, she was part of a large group (25 or so, mostly from San Diego) to whom I was introduced in Phoenix, as we gathered for lunch and headed off to do one of the defining moments in any trail runner's life: the strike-you-dumb Rim-to-Rim-to-Rim—the double crossing of the Grand Canyon. South Rim to North Rim and back to South Rim, without a night's rest at the North Rim hotel.

Whenever I meet someone named Vanessa, it nudges a painfully sweet memory from long ago of a pretty, achingly charming girl with buck teeth who was one of my counselees in a juvenile hall, back when I worked for a street counseling center during my mid-20s. She was in there for having sex at every opportunity with any guy that happened to be available.

One evening, in a private counseling session in a room with a lot of big window glass out onto the hall, she told me, "I know it's just sex to them, but for that short moment, I feel loved, and it's worth all the trouble it causes." I wanted to say, "Please, Vanessa, look me up when you reach adulthood," but I was afraid I would lose my job if I said that.

For years, I looked in vain for a woman who wanted to be loved that much. The wait and the buck teeth would easily have been worth it. And, of course, buck teeth can be straightened, if only someone had cared enough for Vanessa to pay for that. But no one had.

A bunch of us went out in a big van just before sunset to check out the South Kaibab trailhead from which we would be jumping off into the daunting spectacle of the Grand Canyon the next morning. While the rest of us were contemplating our overwhelming destiny of the morrow, Vanessa was asking Shacky, her partner in life's adventure, to get a photo of her standing on one foot, the sole of her other foot pressed against her knee, hands pointed overhead in the yoga posture called "the tree", on a pinnacle that jutted out from the wall of the Canyon with empty air all around.

And it was her idea to have Shacky stand beside the sign warning us that people die here every year, with Shacky imitating the posture and expression of the near-to-death hiker plodding upward on the sign's graphic. And then we all gathered around that sign and imitated that appearance. Little did we know that we would see—and feel—that expression a lot during the upcoming 19 to 20 hours.

Vanessa was checking out the wind-battered trees, the moss, spotting a California Condor on a pinnacle a little ways away, and then jogging down the trail switchbacks in the dusk so far that we called after her, worried she would disappear into the darkness. Whatever we did, wherever we went, take a look around and Vanessa was the one having the most fun. She has seriously decided to enjoy life as much as life can be enjoyed.

That evening at dinner, I was seeking cohorts to join me in an against-the-grain endeavor. Before I had joined them in Phoenix, it had been decided that all of the double-crossing runners (about half of our group just ran to the River and Phantom Ranch and back out) would leave at 3:30 a.m. I wanted to leave at first light because, although I am an acknowledged expert at spectacularly graceful falling, the potential drop on some of those switchbacks was not within my continuum of adaptable risk. Plus, I wanted to see the dawn break over the Canyon.

I was going from table to table at dinner, not having much luck, until Vanessa piped up, "I'd like to do it that way." Then she looked at Shacky (known to his mother as Robert Shackelford) and said, "Is that okay?" And Shacky responded with something like, "Yeah. Sure. I'm in." Then we set about persuading Christine Bilange, who was sporting a cast from breaking her forearm just above the wrist a month earlier in a trail running fall, that she should go down with us in the light of day, when the risk of falling would be greatly lessened.

Five a.m. Vanessa is contagious (as you will find) and we soon were oohing and aahing about half as much as she was over the scenery, and were exquisitely happy to be doing something so magnificent. We were like tourists, except that we ran from ooh and ah to photo op, instead of trudging. It was a weekend in early May, the best time of the year for the Rim-to-Rim-to-Rim double crossing, and wave after wave of runners from all over America came down the trail behind us, saying hi as they passed.

About 15 miles into that day, it started heating up and Shacky started having problems on the long gradual uphill along Bright Angel Creek. His genes are from cool foggy Ireland, and are still having trouble adjusting to the American Southwest. Christine was an uphill demon with genes from the Sun Coast of southern France, and forged ahead, with me following as best I could with my Norwegian-British genes.

As Vanessa writes, she is heavier than the typical ultrarunner (while still being seriously attractive, I might add). I half expected her to melt in the heat, but her Central American genes were having a play day. She and Shacky came into the Pump House rest stop at the base of the brutally gorgeous climb (about 5,500 feet) to the North Rim just as I was leaving a few minutes behind Christine. Shacky flopped down on a bench, looking like a deathly ill man trying out his casket. Vanessa looked like she had just come in off a half-mile walk. "He has trouble with heat and altitude," she explained. I thought, "Oh, Lord! And we've only gone 16 of 44 miles, and not yet done either of the two humongous climbs."

During the remainder of our 19 and 20 hours in that wonderland of stone and sun and air and wind and cold and heat, 19 miles of which was spent in moderate-to-baking temps with the cool Bright Angel Creek tinkling along, tantalizingly nearby, I would become impressed by three astounding phenomena: how much I had to wait for Christine as she tip-toed warily down the switchbacks, and how old and fat and slow she made me feel on the climbs; how Shacky kept looking like death warmed over, yet somehow kept staggering into the longer-and-longer rest stops that I was taking, just as we were about to leave (with Christine—a French dominatrix if there ever was one—calling out, "Okay, Gordy, it's time to go!"); and how Vanessa would, incredibly, run in ahead of Shacky at each of those rest stops to spend some time with Christine and me before going back to pick up Shacky. It even got to where, as the sun got low in the west, I could tell the miles were taking their toll on Vanessa when she started looking like she was coming in off a dusty 10K.

Shacky's devolution from looking like one of the Corps to looking like one of the corpses had progressed so relentlessly by Cottonwood Camp (mile 28 out of 44) that, when Christine and I got to Phantom Ranch (mile 35 of 44), I made arrangements for Shack to have an emergency bed in the bottom of the Canyon. Then we said good-bye to Vanessa (who had run ahead to spend time with us... again!), and headed down to the river, across the bridge, and up 5,000 feet in nine miles. So I wasn't hanging out down by the Colorado River to witness the balancing of Shacky and Vanessa's relationship, when the cool of evening swept through the Grand Canyon, and his Irish genes woke up and said, "Cool, man, cool!", and her tropical genes said, "What is this B.S.? We don't do this!"

So as Christine and I did switchback after switchback into the colder and colder, windier and windier South Rim, we saw a miracle in the darkness far below us: two lights, making their way upward.

Somehow, I feel that this book emerged from those two lights slowly working their way up out of that very deep darkness.

There are those who will find this book to be entertainment. Others will use this book as a bridge to a world they could never have imagined for themselves. In either event, I expect you will agree with me when I say that I wanted this book to linger with me longer. I wanted to spend more time with Vanessa in each place her destiny touched the Earth, which I guess will just have to wait until she writes her next book.

After returning to his life in England after WWI, T. E. Lawrence (of Arabia) wrote *Seven Pillars of Wisdom*, in which he penned: "Most men dream by night, and wake in the day to find that it was vanity. But the dreamers of the day are dangerous men, for they will work their dream with open eyes to make it possible."

I find myself wondering what would have happened if Lawrence had come to know Vanessa as Shacky has come to know Vanessa, and found his kindred spirit. Maybe Lawrence would not have had to ride his motorcycle faster and faster until the end.

Who knows? Maybe the reincarnationists have the right explanation for how the Universe works, and Vanessa is Lawrence of Arabia in our time. At the very least, their spirits know each other well.

And now they both have written a book to show us where to look, should we choose to follow their footsteps, each in our own way.

Vanessa Runs

Introduction

If you're after a book about how to run faster, how to reach a new PR, or how to train for your next race, this is the wrong place to look.

My book is about running, but it doesn't tell you what to do. And it's a memoir, but not about somebody famous.

I'm a girl who started running during a time of overwhelming stress and desperation. I'm someone whose life changed through ultra trail running. These are the stories of how running restored me, how it shifted my perspective, and how it healed my wounds.

This book tracks me from my first 5K all the way to finishing my third 100-mile foot race. It weaves in personal anecdotes from my life, and shows how running transformed all aspects of who I am.

My hope is that it will inspire you to see running in a different light. Not as a weight loss or fitness tool, but as a journey in your own personal growth.

I hope that it will inspire you to experiment with your running. To run more trails, or try an ultra. Or to just let the quiet beauty of getting lost on the side of a mountain supersede the urgency of PRs and race stats. There is so much more to running than what we have often made of it.

In these pages, I face a mountain lion. I struggle with divorce. I quit my job. I'm terrified by suicide. And I run faster and longer than I ever thought possible.

These are my experiences, my stories, and my life. Today, I live in a Rialta RV with my boyfriend Shacky, our dog Ginger, and our kitty Momma. We travel the country, exploring new trails and racing ultras. You can follow my blog and adventures at vanessaruns.com.

I'd also be thrilled to hear what you think of this book. Please consider leaving a review, or you can email me directly at vanessaruns@gmail.com.

I'm an open book. Literally.

See you on the trails!

Vanessa

"May your trails be crooked, winding, lonesome, dangerous, leading to the most amazing view. May your mountains rise into and above the clouds."

– Edward Abbey

Chapter 1:
Growing Up & Learning to Run

On Deciding to Run Long

When you are the oldest of four sisters, not many things belong to you. You don't get your own room. You don't get your own clothes. And when things go wrong, you're the one who gets the blame.

There are a good six years between me and my next sister, and another six years between her and the next one. Because our ages are so spread apart, I played a strong caretaker role in my family, and grew up with a clan mentality. Putting my own needs first and embracing my individuality was not something that was encouraged: I was there to serve the group.

My decision to train for and run a marathon was one of the first things I did that was just for me. I had always wanted to run a marathon, but never talked about it because the timing was never right. My family had more than its share of dramas, and there was always something going on that required attention, or someone that needed my help.

In 2007, I realized that my time would never come. I would forever be cleaning up messes and running damage control. Nobody was going to put me first.

My training was met with some resistance. No outright opposition, but a negative vibe about the time commitment. It created a rift in my relationship with my boyfriend at the time, and suddenly I became less available to participate in family dramas.

For the first time in my life, I was doing exactly what I wanted and making no apologies for it. I was exploring my full potential, and nothing was more important than that. Along the way, I was accused of being selfish, or thinking I was better than my friends and family. Maybe I was all those things.

But I was also happy.

Running was physically hard for me, but without moral support I felt an additional burden. Running took a sheer force of will. Like something beautiful breaking through rocky terrain. And I fought for it.

There is a lot to read out there on how to physically train for a marathon. But so much of it for me was mental. Believing that my body was capable of running that far. That it was okay to train on my schedule, instead of catering to and adjusting to the chaotic schedules of those around me. And the hardest part—believing that I deserved this accomplishment.

I would eat well when others wouldn't. Go to bed when others were staying up. It got lonely sometimes.

But I kept my eyes on the goal, and it made my victory that much sweeter. When I crossed the finish line at my first marathon, I knew that just as nobody had shared in my pain, no one could now share in my glory. I knew that there was no turning back for me. And that in life there is only one way I could possibly go out now: blazing.

On Self-Esteem

One book from my high school reading list has stuck with me all these years. Fay Weldon's *The Life and Loves of a She-Devil* is an easy fictional read about an unhappy, oppressed housewife who embarks on a mission of revenge against her cheating husband, his mistress, and society in general.

This character's meticulous and obsessive plans transform her from a large, strong, dark woman into a petite, delicate blonde. She essentially turns herself into her husband's mistress, becomes the object of his affection, and then exacts her shocking revenge.

It was an unlikely book for me to attach myself to. I was an obsessive reader in high school, but was never much into fiction. This was the only fiction book I kept around to read over and over again.

I identified closely with the main character. I also felt ugly, fat, and powerless. My father was extremely protective, so I felt oppressed. I wasn't allowed friends or sleepovers or dances. I missed my prom and wasn't allowed to wear shorts or skirts that cut above my knees. I was nice and smart, but awkward and friendless.

The transformation of Weldon's character caught my attention. And I wondered if someday I might also live a different life. If I would ever be glamorous or pretty or happy.

Every time I read this book, I see it differently. I started by sympathizing with the main character, cheering her on and identifying with her frustrations. Then I became angrier in my youth and enjoyed it as a story of revenge. I wished that the people in my life could also be punished, and wondered what I might do to them.

Now I'm reading it again as an ultrarunner, and it seems silly, a lot of drama over nothing. I never used to question why this character would want to physically transform into something more petite, but I now cringe at the thought.

She allows her legs, once strong and long and muscular, to wither into bony white sticks. I imagine that she could have chosen to have been a runner instead. She wanted to be fair, but her darker skin would have allowed her more natural protection for longer runs in the sun. She shortens her height, killing what would have been an impressive stride. Her body was powerful but she chose to become helpless. She was strong and in the end she became weak.

Ultrarunning changes the way you think about yourself. In other words, it tweaks your self-esteem. My writer friend and race director Shelley Viggiano once wrote, "When you finish your first ultra, you are transformed from a weak person to a powerful one. There is nothing in life that feels insurmountable any longer, not once you've willingly wrestled with demons that big. When you know what you are capable of, you can take charge of your life. That's what running ultras did for me."

I suspect that the ultra experience is different for women. We are always so down on ourselves and particularly on our bodies. We're never happy. But ultrarunning challenges our concept of self.

4

I was told once that I'd never be a runner because I could never have a runner's body. It was the opinion of someone I respected, so I believed them.

Today, I still don't have a runner's body. Yet I know I'm a runner. My thighs are thick and my hips are larger than most distance runners. My bum is rounder, and the more miles I run, the rounder it gets. I'm more short than tall. More packed than lean.

My training has made my lower body more muscular and defined, but not smaller. My calves and quads are hard, but not skinny. My boobs won't shrink much either.

I don't know what it's like to run with less weight, but I know that I've run 100 miles without stopping, and with no injuries. So whatever my body is doing, it's something efficient.

The truth is, if you are a woman and you have completed an ultramarathon, or even a marathon, you are in a very small, elite percentage of the general population. Your body has accomplished something athletic. It has done something extraordinary.

To turn around and criticize your body for every dimple or pocket of fat is almost like being saved from a burning plane by a superhero only to tell him his cape doesn't match his socks. Nobody cares about that.

Running has taught me to love my body. It does what I want it to, so in return I must lavish it with love and appreciation. Maybe I don't always take the best race photos. But every angle and curve and dimension serves a purpose.

I am an ultrarunner. All the moving parts work well together. And I feel beautiful.

On Freedom

When my baby sister Emma was learning to ride a bike, I made up a game for her called "I Will Follow You Wherever You Go."

There was only one rule: She would bike and I would follow.

I told her that the whole entire world was there for her and her bike. She could go anywhere she wanted for as long as she wanted (even to China!) and I would follow her so that when she was ready to come home, she could follow me back.

Emma loved this.

I could see in her excited little eyes that she really believed her possibilities were endless. She was so little at the time that she only ended up going around the block with lots of weaving and turning (which added adventure for her, but not much distance). Sometimes she would even bring some food and sit down to eat it, so she could imagine she was traveling much farther.

I loved watching her, because it's not often that you have the opportunity to see the expressions of a person who truly believes in endless possibilities. But although it made me happy watching her, I didn't think that was a feeling I could replicate in my own life. I knew we couldn't really go to China. I had lost faith.

Then I ran my first 100-miler. Something I hadn't even trained for. Something that didn't seem possible. And I started believing again. I signed up for my second 100-mile race, and stopped after 55 miles. But I knew that next time I could do better. I signed up for another one. Maybe, like Emma, I could carry some food and go farther.

When I'm on the trails, I know what Emma felt like. Limitless. Uninhibited. And completely free.

On Perseverance

My first running coach, Michael Andrew, once told me about something he saw while on a safari in Africa. His story stayed with me and its message grew in my mind and in my heart. I think about it when I run, and it gives me strength.

Michael told of watching a cheetah chasing a baby impala. I knew that the cheetah is the fastest land animal in the world, and that the baby impala's fate was sealed.

But then, Michael said, the tiny impala started running in tight, continuous circles. This prevented the cheetah from achieving any kind of speed or distance, paralyzing its greatest strength.

Still the cheetah kept chasing and the impala kept running. Around and around they went. The chase lasted a long time until ultimately, to everyone's astonishment, the cheetah gave up and walked away. The baby impala survived.

I've been an impala at most of the ultras I've run, a mere little creature lining up with the big boys. The underdog. I have no speed or experience, but, like the impala, I have perseverance. Determination. And a spirit of never giving up.

I may not always run fast, but I can run forever. The baby impala taught me that it doesn't matter how small I am. I can run with giants.

On Surviving

Our evolutionary instinct, when faced with a danger or threat, is to run. The best runners were the ones who survived. Today, we have different threats. A stressful relationship. A burdensome family. An abusive history. A haunting past. It was these things that drove me to run. And through running, to survive.

The day I started running was one of my roughest: I literally wanted to run away, so I decided I would indeed run. As I ran, things became clearer. Solutions presented themselves. It suddenly didn't seem so bad. And eventually I ran back home, able to face one more day.

The next day I ran again. And again. I got faster. Stronger. I learned to focus on my future, pounding out plans and dreams every time my feet hit the ground. I would get up early. I saw hundreds of sunrises—each one more magnificent than the one before. I started exploring trails, and lost the fear of getting lost. I ran hills, and began to wonder what lay over the horizon. I learned to be brave.

I bought running shoes. Fuel belts. Anything that would keep me going farther and faster. I hardly took the same route twice. I felt like I owned the city. I ran past office buildings. Through cemeteries. Around the perimeter of the lake. Until I could go no further.

I found hidden trails and towering trees and secluded streams. I ran through wind and snow. I'd sometimes come home drenched in rain and mud, thoroughly exhausted. But my eyes would be bright. Cheeks flushed. Muscles strong. And vision clear.

Today when I run, regardless of what I'm going through, all is well. My life sorts itself out. Ideas are born, and I find the tools to make them reality. My mind races, yet I feel calm. My legs move quickly, yet I am still.

While some run as a social activity, I usually prefer to run alone. While others run to stay healthy, for me it's more like a survival tactic. I run because it makes me invincible. Running taught me to survive. And then it taught me to thrive.

On Winter

I first took up running in the middle of a harsh Canadian winter. While everyone else was bundled up, sipping hot cocoa, and staying indoors, I did the opposite.

I didn't want to stay inside. I was restless and stressed and I needed a way to burn off negative energy, so I went outdoors to face the frigid temperatures and gusty, heartless winds. I ran down to the lake where the weather was the roughest, and that's where I would find myself. At the Toronto Lakeshore in February.

The Lakeshore trail is bustling with activity and tourists in the warmer months. Every summer it's packed with runners and bikers. But in February, nobody walks there. It's nothing more than a long stretch of cold, harsh Canadian winter.

I ran the Lakeshore almost every day for the entire season and I never saw another soul. Such solitude in the heart of an enormous city is unparalleled. I owned that trail.

There's not enough said about winter running. Running in the winter is like not giving up when the road gets hard. It's about willpower and perseverance and being faithful to your sport. Loving your path even when it's ugly.

Yes, it's cold. Unforgivably cold. The cold is what makes it good. Like a coach that keeps you moving. You run because if you walk, you will freeze. It tests your limits. Makes you a hero. Only the strong can tread here.

There's an intimacy in winter running brought about by the rawness of the season. Trees stand naked. Every crack on the road lies exposed. Every flaw on the trail is accentuated. Running this trail taught me to see my own flaws in a different light. Not perfect, but beautiful nonetheless.

There's also a softer side. A sense of reciprocated affection from the elements. Like trust built over time. The winds that once only beat against you in defiance suddenly turn in mercy to push you on when you're wearing thin. The sun's glare that once blurred your vision shifts generously to warm your face. You raise your eyes to scenery so motivational in its brilliance that you struggle to later describe it. And then the moment has passed.

The sights I saw that winter don't exist in other people's memories. The lake still as glass. The sun's reflecting hues of orange and red bouncing off intertwining ice sheets. They don't appear on Flickr. You won't see them in tourist photos or on your co-worker's computer desktop. Because nobody was there.

I imagine that years from now, when I try to remember the reason I run, I will think back on those winter moments. I imagine that in the last stretch of my next race, when my legs are burning and my chest is heaving, I'll feel those bittersweet winds on my face.

I live in San Diego now. The sun graces me year-round, warming my face and my heart in a beautiful city. I run along beaches with palm trees where I see surfers and dolphins and wild seals. I also see the mountains. Stunning wilderness and spectacular trails.

But my beginnings were humble. A big city, a concrete jungle, and a single frozen lake. It was there I learned to love running. Not because it was easy. But because it was hard.

So here's to cold nights and foggy breath. Soft snow and hard ground. And all the best things that winter has to offer before wrapping up another year and starting it all over again—only this time a little better.

On Home

I've never been good at staying put. Or following rules for that matter. There has also been, for most of my life, a deep feeling of restlessness followed by an unshakable feeling of loneliness—sometimes mild, and sometimes strong—that perhaps stems from never having deep roots to a single physical location. When I try to describe what this restlessness feels like, my mind wanders.

I have had countless addresses. Many of them are blurs, some home for only a few weeks. But I believe the key to who I am today lies in the memories of these addresses. What they meant to me, and what they didn't.

Address #1: San Salvador, El Salvador

My dad always told me that he married my mom under a tree. I learned years later that this was a nice way of saying that they had sex in the woods as teenagers and I was accidentally conceived.

My grandmother took care of me while my parents tried to become adults very quickly. And the most adult thing they could think to do was cross a border or two, to give me a fair shot at growing up and telling this story.

When I was two years old my parents passed me off to another family. (It was perhaps appropriate to my nature that my parents uprooted me for a very exciting and very illegal journey north before I even had a chance to form memories.) I was to cross into the United States, and later into Canada as another family's child. My parents had rougher journeys that involved multiple jail experiences and being piled into the trunks of cars.

When I was three, I arrived in Canada and was reunited with my mom. We had to wait for a long time for my dad to make it over to us. By the time I saw him again, I didn't know who he was.

I don't have clear memories of this time, so maybe it didn't affect me. Or maybe I learned before I could read that the only constant thing in this world was change. Different parents, different families, different homes. Maybe I learned to always keep moving.

Address #2: Scarborough, Canada

We lived in an enclosed and very dangerous government housing townhouse complex. This was the first childhood home I remember. Our house was white brick and by the back door I etched in crayon: VANESSA'S HOWSE.

But my restlessness didn't subside. I spent very little time indoors. After my mom died of leukemia, my dad became zombie-like and acted like he forgot we existed. His grief was deep, and to this day I

13

question whether he ever really loved anyone else (though he would marry two more times).

My sister and I would spend the day exploring the neighborhood. We kicked away used heroin needles to get to the playgrounds, and picked piss-smelling dandelions to put in our hair. I once saw a man exposing himself to a bunch of my friends, so I steered my sister away. But I was happy as long as I was discovering new places.

Address #3: Toronto, Canada

My dad remarried and I had a new stepmother named Angela. We all moved out of government housing and into an apartment. I had never lived in an apartment before and I found it suffocating. It was much smaller than our townhouse, and I couldn't understand why we were moving to less space instead of more. Where my dad used to be neglectful, he was now overprotective. I couldn't go outside like I was used to, and sometimes I would feel like the walls were closing in on me. But it didn't take me long to find a new escape—my mind.

I'd lie on my bed and read obsessively. I'd get up in the middle of the night to read or write. I'd keep journals of all the places I wanted to go and the things I wanted to see. I planned my future—career, life, family. Hundreds of different paths. It never occurred to me that I wouldn't have enough lifetimes to fulfill each one.

Address #4: Jane & Finch, Toronto

My parents bought a house in what was considered a dangerous area in Toronto. Moving back into a house was a relief for me. Again, I spent very little time indoors. It was during this time that I discovered biking.

With the bike, my boundaries expanded, and I'd ride with the same awe and exploratory spirit I had as a child. The world was mine to discover, and there was nowhere I couldn't go.

Address #5: Mendoza, Argentina

After my parents divorced, my Toronto home was no longer a place I wanted to come back to. So I married an Argentine I barely knew and went to live in South America with him. In my mind, this was my escape ticket. I was finally traveling, just like I had always wanted to.

But Argentina turned out to be a tiny oppressive room I was barely allowed to leave. It meant never being able to go anywhere alone. And being married meant submission and obedience and visiting his mother every single day. I lasted three months.

Address #6: Toronto motels

I didn't have a home when I came back to Toronto, so I stayed at various cheap motels and moved around until I could gather my thoughts. Moving kept me focused. I could see a goal ahead as long as I wasn't standing still.

Address #7: Etobicoke, Canada

Two older ladies from local churches took me in at different times and let me stay in their spare rooms. But their charity was not entirely free: they wanted me to spend all day inside with them and be their constant company. They resented my restless nature and preference for adventure. They said it wasn't proper. After one too many scoldings, I took off.

Address #8: Lansdowne & Bloor, Canada

This was the kind of intersection where you could buy drugs as soon as you stepped off the subway. It was dark and dirty and people were afraid to go there at night. The room I rented was in a retrofitted house. There were eight bedrooms and only one bathroom. The other tenants were drug dealers and pimps — very mobile individuals. I was the only girl.

In the winter I would freeze and in the summer I would scorch. But for the first time, I didn't have a soul breathing down my neck. I could come and go as a pleased. And I mostly wanted to go.

I practically lived on my bike. I would wake up in the middle of the night and pedal like a madwoman down to the lake, where the road would end. I'd dip my feet in the water, or just lay on the grass for hours until daylight. There was no sense to my wanderings. I simply went where I wanted, when I wanted. Life was good.

I quickly learned not to talk about my adventures, which were constantly met by shock and horror. It wasn't fit for a young woman to wander shady neighborhoods at night. It was wrong to hop fences or dip under bridges. People felt that I should have been more afraid. But I never was.

I developed an extensive inventory of secret spots that became all my own. Places I visited by myself. And corners where, had I died there, my body to this day would still be undiscovered.

Address #9: Downtown Toronto, Canada

This wasn't a great area, but I loved it because it was where I first started to run. It was also close to my school (I got my journalism degree at Ryerson University). In the heart of downtown, at five a.m., I would literally leap over sleeping bums on the street. I'd run through the big business districts and never see them so empty. Running made me feel like the entire city was my playground. Exhilaration is the closest word to describe what I felt.

Address #10: North York, Canada

This condo was the first home I ever owned. It was an upscale building, close to the subway, and had some decent green space nearby. But what sold me on it was the view: floor to ceiling windows along the entire back wall. Winter or summer, I felt like I was outside.

I tried to build my nest here with my (now ex) boyfriend. I painted walls and bought furniture. I worked to make the space welcoming and invited people over.

But I still craved the outdoors. I wanted the wind in my hair, rain against my face, and mud between my toes. From my beautiful home, I would run barefoot to the woods like a crazy person, still looking for those secret spots.

To my boyfriend's distress, I would still wake up in the middle of the night seeking the cover of starlight. His hope and mine had been that with some stability, I could become domesticated. It just wasn't my nature.

Address #11: San Diego, California

I left my boyfriend, packed a single carry-on suitcase, and moved to San Diego in search of more trails and more running. I had no job, no prospects, and no "Plan B." But as soon as I landed, I knew I belonged in California. Within a month, I had a work visa, a steady job, and a new ultrarunner boyfriend named Shacky. I was running mountains and beaches and when people asked me if I had plans to return to Toronto, I couldn't imagine why I would.

Address #12: None

At the age of 29, I said goodbye to my office job as a nutrition editor and focused on the only two things I cared to do: running and writing. I grew dreads and ran mountain trails almost exclusively.

Shacky and I gave up our home and moved into a Rialta RV with our dog Ginger and a stray cat we adopted after finding her pregnant and shivering on our doorstep. We call her Momma. We currently have no permanent address, just a mailbox in South Dakota.

We have several projects going on: more books in progress, and physical challenges like conquering all the 14,000-foot summits in Colorado. I'm busier than ever, yet nothing I do feels like work. My life has finally lined up with what I knew was true all along: Home is the trails I run.

When I'm on the trails, I can be in unknown surroundings yet it still feels familiar. A tree will always be a tree. Earth and ground and sky — these are the constants in my life. Rain and sunshine are recurring events that I can count on year after year. My traditions are the passing of time. The changing of seasons. And like all these things, I am always just passing through.

On My Mother

My mom passed away from leukemia when I was nine and she was only 27. She didn't allow me to see her in the final months, when she was at her worst, so all my memories with her are happy ones. For a long time I struggled with this, and wished I had been given the chance to say goodbye. But I know that even on her deathbed, she did what she thought was best for me. And maybe she was right.

Until the age of nine, my childhood was happy and ideal. It was her upbringing that gave me the strength to deal with the disasters that would follow. My mom taught me to care for my younger sisters. She taught me to read before I was in school. It's because of her that I can write and read and speak fluent Spanish.

My mom taught me to memorize things. We didn't eat junk food and we didn't own a TV. Instead, I played outside and read obsessively. She birthed my loves of learning and nature, which drive me to this day.

My mom also instilled in me a love for food, allowing me to be around the stove and knives when I was as young as five, touching food and creating meals with her. She would dress me up in pretty dresses, then allow me to run outside and play in the mud. Never once did she ever complain about me getting dirty.

Today, there are pictures of me climbing fences with perfect ponytails and scraped knees. She let me run barefoot. My mom would never sit and watch like the other moms. She was right in there with me. Climbing trees or chasing me. My mom was my entire world.

I can't imagine what kind of person I would be today were it not for my mother. I don't think I would have made it. In every crisis I went through, I was always drawing from the strength she instilled in me. My mom was a fighter, just like me. Strong but gentle. Feminine but tough. She wasn't scared of anything and I could never fool her. She knew all my secrets. I think of my mom when I run. When the run gets hard, I imagine her watching me.

On one of the last days that I saw her, my mom called me over to her bed. She gave me a little red Gideon New Testament Bible and told me she wanted me to always read it and live by it. Inside she had written a dedication for me in Spanish. She said she hoped I would base my life on that book.

At the time, I had no way of knowing the value of that last gift from her. Or what she could have been feeling, knowing that it was the last thing she would ever give me. But I did sense some kind of significance and I kept it close by, with my other "important" things.

I did read that Bible. A little bit every day, and sometimes a lot. I read it with a highlighter because I had seen my dad highlight important things. After my mom died, my Bible got put away with my other books and moved around a lot as I kept changing locations. I had very few possessions at this time since I had no real home. Every time I moved I would leave things behind, until finally I had nothing. But the Bible stayed with me.

Today, the Bible pages are worn and bent. The front page where my mom wrote her dedication is ripped. But every single word in that Bible is highlighted.

My mom died on Valentine's Day 1990. My dad told me that God needed a Valentine and he had picked the prettiest one. I never questioned that.

At the funeral I wore a blue and black dress. It was an open casket and the first time I had ever seen a dead body. I wasn't scared because it didn't look like the person lying there was my mom. She had a lot of makeup on, which my mom never wore. Her face was white and powdered instead of her usual olive skin and rosy cheeks. I touched her hand and her face. She was cold and rubbery. I didn't cry.

Grieving for me is like something that never goes away. It doesn't really hurt anymore, but it's always there. Like an invisible scar. I find that at each stage of my life I miss her differently and for different reasons. Things I wanted to ask her that I ended up learning the hard way. Or situations I could have avoided if she had just been there to point me along. Milestones in my life that I wish she could have seen. Moments where she might have been proud of me.

I was alone for so long without her. But I remember her when I run. This is my way of keeping her close.

On My First 16 Miles

When I started training for my first marathon, 16 miles seemed like an insane distance. If you had told me back then that I would someday run 100 miles, I would have choked on my own gel. Here is what I wrote after running 16 training miles for the first time, a major milestone for me:

***

The sky looked ominous when I woke up this morning. There was no sun in sight. The streets were empty and dark and grey. A thick fog hung stubbornly over the entire landscape visible from my balcony, threatening rain. I couldn't help smiling excitedly. The perfect morning for a run.

I went to bed early last night in preparation for my big day, so I was surprised to find that an unusually large number of emails had come in overnight. Comments on my blog, wishing me luck. Emails with inspirational quotes or mantra suggestions. Videos posted to my Facebook page. Links sent to me through Facebook messages. I read them all.

After that I slipped into my black running skirt and a pair of socks. I put on my bright yellow race shirt from the Acura Toronto 10-miler and pulled back my hair. I grabbed my water and my keys, and headed out.

The sun started coming out gradually. The fog slowly lifted and traffic started to build. By that time, I was thinking about mantras. Someone left a comment on my Facebook page that said:

Mantra: Be present. Do not miss what is happening right now. You are not running 22K, you are simply running and enjoying all your perception is creating. I decided my mantra for today would be, BE PRESENT. I liked that.

I had decided to run along my marathon route, following the same path that I would face in October. The marathon start line is only two blocks from my house, so I jogged there. Then I began.

I thought hard about being in the present, and looked around for details along the route. I paid attention to the grooves in the road and the various inclines. I tried to memorize where I might be able to pass people on race day, and where I was better off keeping a steady pace. I imagined how the area might look with the roads closed and packed with runners.

The first 10K was the hardest. It was all uphill, and by the time it was over I had finished almost all of my water.

I had started at Yonge & North York Centre Blvd. The marathon route would take me straight down Yonge Street.

On marathon day, I would run to the point where Yonge Street ends, at the Toronto Lakeshore. I've been there a million times, but I had never run there from my house. Today I was only scheduled to run to Yonge & Rosedale, exactly eight subway stops away. By subway, this trip would take me about 20 minutes.

I hit Yonge & Sheppard, subway station #1. No big deal. The run to subway station #2, York Mills, was harder.

Be present, be present. I kept reminding myself. So I started to look around. I was crossing a bridge with a highway entrance nearby. Traffic zoomed past me on one side as I struggled along the sidewalk. On the other side, there were rusted out metal borders and a fence preventing me from falling into an overgrown army of what looked like itchy bushes.

Along the side of those bushes I spotted a yellow plant that grows all over the city. You always find it in the company of weeds and dandelions. Unkempt places where dogs go to pee.

When I was a child, my grandmother would take me out to collect this plant. She would bring me to an overgrown field and tell me to pick as many as I could. She said it was good for tea.

I never knew what this plant was called and I haven't thought about it since then. When we'd get back to my grandmother's house, she would boil these and drink the tea. I never had any because I was told I was too young for tea. I was just the plant picker.

Trying to remember what my grandmother had called this plant and wondering if I had picked any that dogs had urinated on, pushed me through my first hill.

I was at Yonge & Lawrence, subway station #3.

Lawrence is the station I exited last Christmas for a church concert with my sister Emma and other family members. The first choir group that sang was not very good. Actually, they basically killed music. But they meant well. God bless them.

One of the group members sang something that he had written himself and it was so bad I had to bury my face in my hands and pretend to pray in order to stop my body from convulsing with laughter.

Emma was better behaved than I was, but we still couldn't look at each other through the entire repertoire. The song was so repetitive that it was stuck in my head for an entire week. On the way home, Emma and I sang it and it became our new favorite.

I was now at Yonge & Eglinton. Subway #4.

This is where I went to nutrition school. It's congested and close to downtown. The homeless stake their claims on several warm grates, and the shortest distance from the subway to my school would lead me straight through a smelly homeless man's bedroom. The smell was a mixture of PineSol and body odor.

He was always sleeping when I passed, and whenever I headed to class I had to decide whether or not I wanted to risk waking him, or take a longer route instead. I always felt apologetic as I passed; I was intruding on his home.

There was a time when I would befriend the homeless. In high school, I was convinced that when I had my own apartment I would have a mob of homeless people living with me. Then I moved out and rented a room in a run-down complex where it was me and (wouldn't you know it!), several homeless drug addicts. I was the only girl and there were no locks on the showers. It wasn't as idyllic as I had imagined.

When I was 17, I regularly stopped to talk to a homeless man that I saw on my way home. His name was Gord. I bought him a pizza once with some money I had saved up and we ate it together. He showed me his journal and he gave me a poem that he had written. I memorized it:

I drank to ease this endless pain
Of my awful childhood days
Those rotten people who abused me
I let those painful memories get in my way
I had my first taste of alcohol at 16
And I loved the feeling it gave
I never dreamed 30 years later
It would be leading me to my grave
You've probably seen me sitting on a sidewalk
Foam cup in my hand
Expecting passerbys to give money
To this employable, but hurting man
Many a time I have woke up on a dirty sidewalk
Hungover, lonely, cold, hungry, and sore
My t-shirt still soaked with the tears
That I cried the night before
I have no fear when I'm drinking
I'm not even afraid to die
But I'm terrified of everything when I'm sober
Especially the need to cry
- Gord Atkinson

I got home that day and my dad punished me because I was late. I never told him about Gord. Gord disappeared one week after that. I called the number he had left me, but it was disconnected.

Yonge & Davisville. Subway #5

I now ran alongside my favorite cemetery. This has been my escape many times. I've run here, biked here, walked here, photographed here, or just hung out. Always alone.

Mount Pleasant cemetery is a place of solitude for me. It's enormous and green, with tons of strange birds and little bugs that I can't identify. I like looking at the graves. And I wonder things.

I wonder about the expensive stones, and how much they cost. I wonder about the people who don't have a stone at all, and if anyone visits them. I wonder if anyone got to write their own inscriptions, or what happened to all their assets.

I wonder where the most visited grave is. Which deceased person was most loved. Who had the biggest funeral. Who had the person they love fail to show up. I wonder what is the most valuable object buried in these coffins. Which has the most significance. And why. I wondered whether any other runner wonders these important things when they pass this place.

Yonge & St. Clair. Subway #6.

This was the location of my very first job when I was a teenager. It took a lot to convince my dad to allow me to work and the only reason he agreed was because my aunt worked here, and she would be working with me.

I would get off at St. Clair to walk to a senior's residence a couple of blocks away. This was a very upscale senior's home, where everyone pretended that nobody gets sick and nobody dies and nobody has been abandoned at all.

I worked in the restaurant. The function of it was more like a cafeteria, but the appearance of a restaurant was an important part of the illusion. It was my job to make old people believe that this was an upscale, very expensive restaurant. Except nobody had to bring them a bill.

The seniors would dress up and make outrageous demands. They would send food back and complain until they were blue in the face. They would treat the servers badly and sometimes they would even have temper tantrums.

My aunt was always stressed and flustered, but I was the youngest so nobody really expected much of me. I was there because of my aunt and because they didn't have time to hire anyone better. I wasn't particularly happy.

After dinner I would sneak into the fridge and drink milk. A lot of milk. Sometimes I would even bring milk home. Sometimes I would finish all the milk in the fridge.

There was never enough food at home and I was always hungry, so serving food all day was tough. Milk was my revenge. They eventually fired me, of course. But at least it wasn't because of the milk.

Yonge & Summerhill. Subway #7.

This was the location of the church that I grew up in. They had a building right across the street from the subway exit. Real estate here was expensive, so the building was tiny. My years at this church came and went with not much significance. Except for my best friend.

Her name was Silvia. She was from Panama and we were an unlikely pair. She was a beautiful child. A big mess of curly hair. Big brown eyes. Olive skin.

My skin was lighter. My hair was stringy and unkempt. And whatever eyes I had were hidden behind a bright orange pair of old woman spectacles which my dad had picked out of a church donation bin and forced me to wear. Still, for some reason, Silvia worshipped me.

On the weekends we would play. She was into Barbies and I was more into *anything* else, so we would compromise: I'd play Barbies with her, and then she had to go outside and do whatever I told her. I was always the "smart" one. And Silvia was the "pretty" one.

I secretly wanted to be the pretty one, so once in a while I would get passive-aggressive on her. Make her do stupid things to amuse me. Then one day I found out that she had begged her mom for a pair of glasses like mine. I could not compute this. When I confronted her about it, she said she wanted to be just like me. I told her she had lost her mind.

One day Silvia was pissing me off and I really wanted to hit her. But I knew that I would be in such big trouble that it almost wasn't worth it. So instead I instigated her to hit me, knowing that she would be gravely punished.

She hit me a little sooner (and much harder) than I had planned, knocking me right in the nose with the rock hard face of a Cabbage Patch doll. I shot my hand up to my nose, stunned to find it gushing blood. Silvia screamed and ran out the door, still clutching the bloody doll. Her mother brought her back, dragging her by the hair and beating her with a belt. That was a messy day.

Yonge & Rosedale! I can see it!

My legs feel strong, lost in thought. My breathing is steady. The light is red—a perfect opportunity for me to turn around and head home. There's a park right at Rosedale. I was planning to loop around it before heading back. The park is on my right and the subway entrance is on the left.

The light changes to green, and my path to the park is now blocked. So I keep going.

***

My high school English teacher gave us an assignment once. This was for an enriched English class. Being enriched meant that we didn't have to respect the normal curriculum. We watched movies in class and discussed issues in the media. We were encouraged to think critically instead of just memorizing Shakespeare. And we wrote a lot—an essay a day. It was heaven.

For one particular assignment, we had to watch *Gattaca*, a 90s sci-fi movie with Uma Thurman and Ethan Hawke. In this movie, almost every newborn child is genetically altered to form a mentally and physically superior human being based on exceptional DNA formulas.

There was a family with two brothers. One of the brothers was genetically altered to be superior. The other brother was not. Every summer, the brothers would play together near the ocean. They had a game.

They challenged each other to swim out as far as each of them dared. The first one to turn back was the loser.

Time after time the genetically inferior brother would turn back. Until one day, he just kept swimming. They went farther and farther until finally the genetically modified brother turned back. That was the last time they ever raced.

Years later the weaker brother confessed the reason he had won that race all those years ago. It was simple. "I didn't save anything for the way back."

And that's what I think about now. About not saving anything for the way back.

About going... until I can't.

Yonge & Bloor.

Yonge & Wellesley.

Yonge & College.

Yonge & Dundas.

Then I turn around, and think for a second... what have I done? Have I gone too far? Will I ruin my training? I don't have any money for the subway, so I start running home.

College.

Wellesley.

Bloor.

Rosedale.

It's not as bad as I imagined. Running home is always easier.

Summerhill.

St. Clair.

Davisville.

Eglinton.

I know what's waiting for me, and that spurs me on. Air conditioning. A shower. Clean clothes. Lunch.

Lawrence.

York Mills.

Sheppard.

And North York Centre.

I'm home. I can't believe it! Back to family and friend and familiarity. Comfort and relaxation. My hardwood floors and my oak table and my balcony. And all those other intangible things—the ones that make home a worthy destination.

I'm surrounded by things that swell me with the courage and the strength to run away in the first place. Knowing that I will always come back. That coming home will always be easier.

On Food

When I was in nutrition school, one of my instructors was an eccentric elderly lady with grey hair, thin lips, and a pointed nose. She wore patterned head wraps with beaded jean jackets and flowing, brightly-colored skirts. But she had a stern face and a no-nonsense personality.

She would always ask us whether the comments we made in class were coming from love or from fear. I didn't always understand what she was talking about, and I was a little bit scared of her. But she changed the way I look at nutrition.

On the first day of class, she asked us to come up with two words to describe our relationship with food.

Some people used words like confused, complicated, obsessive, or passionate. Mine were: analytical and inquisitive.

After we had shared our words, she asked us to think about our lives in general, and see whether those words could also be used to accurately describe ourselves. It was a perfect fit for everyone in the room.

Her point was that food is intimately connected to who we are. We are what we eat. Or at least, we relate to life the same way we relate to food. I never forgot that.

Since then, I have discovered other links between my life and my diet. I've noticed that my mindset when I run is similar to my mindset when I eat.

When I became my sister Elizabeth's nutritionist, we explored this body-mind connection in her nutritional assessment. About her relationship with food, she wrote: "Eat when you can because there might not be food later."

Because we were raised together, I understand what she's talking about. I knew growing up that I had to gorge whenever possible, and save as much food as I could for later. After our mom passed away, our fridge was always empty and we could go days without a proper meal. I was always hungry, but the worst part was worrying about my baby sister Elizabeth. At church, I would tear apart the cupboards when no one was looking, trying to find something edible for her.

Food continued to haunt me. In university, I signed up to volunteer at a food bank in the hopes that maybe I could swipe a can or two. I was too embarrassed to actually use the food bank. My lowest point came in my second year when, extremely hungry and strapped for cash, I picked up the leftover pizza crusts discarded on the tables of the school cafeteria, and shamefully ate them.

I've been good at saving things all my life, and not just food. When I'm running, I prefer to save my energy, save my breath, and pace myself. That's why I'm better suited to longer distances, but terrible at speed work. I'm always thinking about preserving strength for later.

When I do interval or plyometric training, I run into trouble. I'm not used to giving everything I have. I automatically hold back and try to save my energy. The reason behind that is fear. Fear that I won't be able to finish. That my energy will run out and never come back. That I might hurt myself. And yes—that there will not be enough food to refuel.

Over time, I have learned to let go. I have come to understand that my strength will always come back, and it's okay to exhaust it sometimes. I know now that I'm in a safe place and can trust my environment. I can give it my all and push as hard as possible.

My love of running helped me overcome these mental and emotional barriers. Now I appreciate every meal on my table and all the food in my belly. I take great comfort in knowing that no matter how long my race is, there will always be food at the next aid station.

On Inspiration

My gym trainer in Toronto once made up a workout from hell based on a life-and-death sport played by the ancient Mayans.

If you've seen the movie *The Road to El Dorado*, you might remember an interpretation of it there. The game was a cross between soccer and basketball and was played with a very heavy ball. The winners would become heroes. The losers would be killed as human sacrifices. Fairly decent incentive.

When the Mayan jails became full, all the inmates would be put on a team against the reigning champions. If they won, not only were they given their freedom, but they were treated like kings. If they lost: capital punishment. The original *Hunger Games*.

This game involves quick movements. Throwing and running at full power. So my trainer gave me a heavy medicine ball. I would throw it to her as hard as I possibly could, and with the same momentum I would take off into a sprint. I would also have to throw it with the same force while doing long side leaps, and catch it again. After that I would throw it across the gym and chase it. I almost hit a few people in the head, but as my trainer said, "They should watch where they're going!"

The ancient Mayan culture revolved around this sport. It was usually held in a stadium, gladiator-style. So my trainer had me do my entire workout in front of the long row of treadmills, where everyone could watch me. This actually helped me move faster and not give up. It's hard to stop when people are staring you down.

These workouts were always difficult for me. But if I started getting discouraged, my trainer would tell me Mayan anecdotes, and I would find inspiration. The rich history of sport drove me to dig deep and find my inner Mayan.

On Barefoot Running

When people talk about barefoot running, they tend to discuss things like heel strikes and mid-food landings and foot anatomy. But other foot facts tell a more exciting story:

- The network of nerves that stimulate your feet are the same network that are present in your genitals. The sensory neurons in your feet are so powerful that a minor tickle can send your entire body into an uncontrollable spasm.
- The sensation on your feet is equivalent to the sensation on your lips and fingertips.
- Only your face and hands compare to your feet when it comes to delivering instant sensory messages to your brain.
- Our pulse is very easily felt on specific parts of the body that are also linked with sensual pleasure. Our necks. Our wrists. Our genitals. And the pulse can be felt in not one, but two spots in our feet: the Dorsal Pedis Artery and the Posterior Tibial Artery.

One is at the ankle and the other on the top base of your foot. These are your pressure points.

Yes, running barefoot helps with form. Yes, it helps with injury. But it also feels so damn good! The sensual combinations are hard to ignore.

Sensitive toes standing on a bed of dried pine needles. Soft flesh pressed up against the rough bark of an old tree. The contrast of clear olive skin against the bright red of the leaves and rich browns of the dirt. Warm toes digging into cool, fresh soil. Flushed cheeks from both the crisp cold air and the sweaty exertion of running. Just the right amount of dirty.

Running barefoot can clarify relationships. It teaches us the most important qualities in any partner: not a scholar, not a millionaire, but someone who can move gracefully and efficiently in their natural environment. Someone who can see a destination, know all the routes towards it, and pick the most scenic one. Someone who is not afraid of planting their feet on the ground or taking some pain. Just the right amount of wild.

Running barefoot is like experiencing the world for the first time. It's all about experimentation and discovery. Different surfaces. Different conditions. Different times of day. Track, treadmill, grass, concrete, and mud. It inspires a strong mental connection to the physical act of running. It grounds you. Forces you to be in the moment. Your mind doesn't wander and you don't miss a single thing along the way.

When I run barefoot, my instincts come alive. It's like I have an extra sense. I'm sharply aware of every crack in the pavement, every pebble on the ground, every animal that senses me. I can almost hear the neural connections in my brain as I run over different textures. Like I am just now understanding the difference between cold and hot. Hard and soft. Smooth and rough.

There is something to be said about barefoot pain in the right amounts. How can we know pleasure without pain? Pain encourages treading softly and stepping gently. Then when you step on a pebble or your calf pulls a little or you feel your hair brushed roughly by a branch as you whiz past, it's like a rough kiss. An unexpected nibble on your lower lip. A pull that calls forth a small surge of anger, infusing a mild sense of aggression into each following movement. A perfect blend of pleasure and pain.

I've always been a barefooter at heart. I like the feeling of rubbing dirt between my toes. I feel like an extension of nature, like a branch or a blade of grass, in many ways dependent on the trails I tread.

There's a sense of being simultaneous aware of the details as well as the big picture. I can hear which trees rustle which leaves. I know whether the movements around me are caused by the wind or something living. At the end of my run, my pupils are sharp, bright, and fully dilated. I am a wild animal.

On Spirituality

Although I grew up in the Baptist church, my inquisitive nature kept me on the outskirts. For example, a pastor once told me I could not join his church because I asked too many questions.

But there were other things that bothered me. Nothing more so than a sense of victimization that plagued the congregation. Religion was used as an excuse to blame an outside force for our maladies. Example—It must have been God's will that I got diabetes. Nothing at all to do with years of poor diet and lack of exercise.

Whatever happens to us, we are not responsible. It was God's will. We were not driven to improve ourselves.

If we are sick, we pray. But we rarely eat better. Or exercise. Or rest. Or make any change to our lifestyle. We sit and wait for God to heal us. And if our health does improve, we delve right back into our unhealthy lifestyles.

Right after University, I was accepted into a Master's program at a Baptist seminary. There has always been a spiritual dimension to my life, and I was hoping seminary would help me sort it out. But the seminary building itself felt lifeless and empty. It was like walking into a mall instead of a sacred place.

The seminary was located in a place that was nearly impossible to access without a car. At the time, I was used to walking everywhere or riding my bike. Walking would make me feel more grounded and closer to the earth. I would even grocery shop on my bike, often riding back to my apartment carrying vegetables on my back. But I felt out of place in seminary. So isolated. There was no place to buy fresh food. No trees to shade me at lunch.

When I dropped out, I interpreted that failure as a personal spiritual defect. I wasn't Christian enough to get it. Or deep enough to understand. I was just someone who wanted to be barefoot and eat food that was grown in the ground and sit under a tree. It wasn't enough to be spiritually enlightened.

But now I wonder, what if that was enough?

The Bible says that perfect love drives out fear, and that God is love. So in our pursuit of love, we should be fearless. We learn that every choice we make is fueled by either faith or fear, and to make decisions based on fear is a violation of faith.

And yet religion often plays around some sort of fear. "Do this… or else." Fear that the world will end. Fear that we won't convert enough people. Fear that nobody will come to our churches. Fear that there won't be enough money to pay the pastor.

But in nature, I'm not afraid of anything. My spirit is calm and I feel that if I only stood still for long enough, I could feel God's breath on the back of my neck. Like the ground itself is holy. I've never felt that way in a church.

I don't have it all figured out, but I'm going to keep looking. Not in a seminary, but in the woods.

On My First 30K

Preparations for my first 30K distance — a training run for my marathon — began the night before. I love when my runs are planned thoroughly, so I prepared for this one the way that I would a race. I laid out all my clothes, mapped out my route, prepared my drinks and my keys and my shoes, and I cleaned my entire house from top to bottom. (I'm not sure why the cleaning is important to me, but it's part of my ritual.)

I actually went to bed before the sun. I didn't set an alarm because I wanted to wake up naturally, feeling rested. I didn't want to fall out of bed, shaken awake by an alarm clock, dreading what 30K would feel like. I wanted to open my eyes and think, "YESS!! This is the day!"

It was strange falling asleep with the setting sun still piercing through my blinds. But also calming. Everything was clean and quiet, so I buried my head into my blankets to block out the light, and immediately fell asleep.

I dreamed about running. I saw myself starting out on my 30K, in unknown surroundings. As I fell into a steady pace, I noticed that in the distance a group of people had gathered. A handful of young, flirty girls wearing bikinis loitering around a bunch of young men in their swimming shorts, hanging off each other and laughing. They were coming up from a long set of stairs leading straight down to a sandy beach, as if they had just finished a party and were stumbling home. The sound of crashing waves captured my curiosity, so I decided to explore. I hadn't known there was a beach there.

I descended the stairs to find a large empty beach and an endless ocean. I looked up at the sand, and gasped. There, spanning a distance of approximately half a mile, were the largest, most breathtaking sand sculptures I had ever seen.

Giant sand-women with legs disappearing into the water were sprawled across the beach as if tanning. A sand-woman a short distance away was completely naked, lying artistically on one side with a sly smile and erect nipples. Near her lay yet another naked woman on her back, her sand-hair spread out majestically for several yards. A perfectly chiseled sand-man was stretched out on top of her, his fingers delicately intertwining her hair and his face buried into her neck.

Everything looked real. Carved out at impossible angles. Defying gravity with every curve. Then the tide came in and the sculptures were immediately washed away. Every last one of them. I sighed and wondered whether anyone would ever believe what I had seen. I was about to climb the stairs and continue my run when I saw the retreating tide was starting to raise the sands again.

Out of nowhere, sand-shapes began to take form, climbing out from under the tide. Big lumps at first, and then some of the sand would fall away to reveal identifiable shapes. They were animals. Just as enormous as before, and all different kinds. Huge crabs. Towering seals. Horses and birds. The tide kept rushing the shore, and every time it retreated a new animal would form underneath it, carved out in great detail. Every shell. Every hair follicle. Every blowhole. Then they started to move.

First the seals. Then the bears. The crabs started clicking their claws and huge water snakes formed and slithered quickly across the ground at my feet. I looked up into the water and from the tide itself: white belugas made of sand were playing in the waves.

This happened several times. With each new tide came new creatures. And I realized that this beach would never stop. This was its nature. And that some parts of the world were still magical.

It was this realization that woke me up. I slipped into my clothes, pulled my hair back, and started to run.

On Trees

Remember the exhilaration of climbing trees when you were a kid? That thrill is still there. Much like sprinting through a dewy meadow or rolling down a hill, it's impossible to climb a tree without laughing or grinning. When I first started running trails, I couldn't resist the beautiful trees in my forest and I climbed them every chance I got.

Many of us spend all day trapped in a disconnect between our bodies and our minds: our bodies are in one place while our minds are wandering elsewhere. But when you're climbing, your mind and body are working in unison. Everything is pulling in one direction: up.

I climb trees barefoot. There's something about scaling a tree in bare feet that makes me very happy. The rough bark under my toes. Pushing my body up against gravity. Leaves brushing against my face and arms. That doesn't happen at the gym.

Climbing trees is harder than it looks. It requires the use of muscles that aren't normally isolated in mainstream strength workouts. I like to consider myself a fairly fit person, but I am sore after a day of climbing trees.

For me, the climbing is about learning to move in my natural environment with grace and strength. At first, I'm clumsy and awkward. But over time I slowly learn to slip into a tree more naturally. I learn how to grab the bark, wrap my legs around the base, and shuffle up. Then shuffle down.

Once I scaled a tree, sat up there quietly, and watched a man and his dog walk underneath me. The man didn't notice me (nobody ever looks up!), but the dog picked up on something strange. He sniffed around a bit and... looked up. Then he started barking furiously at the foot of my tree. The man looked and I know he saw me, but he pretended not to. (It's always best to ignore the strange human in a tree.)

The best part about climbing is the thrill that suddenly hits you. At one point your mind catches up to what you're doing and you feel scared. Maybe you glance down. Maybe you realize that you have no idea how to get down. Or you see a big fat spider. Whatever the reason, at a certain point you feel a tingle followed by a rush of scary.

This is often the point where I climb down. But I come back another day. I'll climb the same tree again, and this time I go a little farther. Sometimes I'll do this over many days. Until I'm not afraid anymore.

On Music

My old gym trainer once told me I was a tough person to motivate. My physical performance was very dependent on my frame of mind, and there was little she could do or say to tweak my state. Some days I went to the gym thinking, "I've got this!" and I'd break my own records. Other days I'd come in neutral, or unsure, and I'd regress.

I've been a nerd all my life; it's hard for me to believe sometimes that I can also compete as an athlete. But music is one of the things that can drive me.

Some of my favorite songs remind me of where I've come from and where I'm going. And a song needs to have personal meaning to motivate me.

I can't use running songs off other people's playlists. It's like trying to run with a shoe that's two sizes too small and the lace is missing. It's not enough for a song to have a running beat. For me, it has to have a history.

Growing up, I wasn't allowed to listen to secular music, so I tried my best to learn about the world through the music I had. Christian artists like Steve

Green and Michael W. Smith were part of my childhood era.

My mom loved the song, *He Who Began a Good Work* by Steve Green. They even played it at her funeral. I remember thinking it made the worst possible funeral song because it talks about how God will complete the work He has started in someone. My mom died of cancer at age 27. So at her funeral, I wondered: what is complete about this?

I wondered that for many years, and listened to that song over and over again, as if it would help me uncover some clue about why my mom had to die. One day on a run I was listening to it and thinking about all the good my mom brought into my life, and how her lessons helped me cope with all the difficulties that followed. And it dawned on me—maybe the work being completed wasn't in her. Maybe it was in me.

When my now ex-boyfriend was involved in a serious work accident that put him in a coma, I entered one of the darkest times of my life. Friends turned their backs on me, and people blamed me for his accident. Although I wasn't there when it happened, many claimed I was a curse in his life. My own father, who I hadn't seen in a long time, made a single trip to the hospital to tell me God was going to kill him because I was a sinner. My runs in those days were fueled by the singer Pink, and I played her song *18 Wheeler* over and over again. It helped me cope.

Other songs provoke fonder memories. Like Ronan Keating's *I Hope You Dance*. This song reminded me of growing up with my baby sister, wandering our streets, looking for places to play. We'd pick the weeds along the parking garage and bring them home as flowers. Today, this song reminds me to still see the world in that light. To find wonder in the weeds.

Running for me is the physical and emotional act of moving forward. Leaving all the garbage behind and striving toward a better future. And never looking back.

On Hopelessness

My baby sister Emma was barely in high school the first time she overdosed on drugs. When she was 14, she started cutting her arms. The overdose wasn't Emma's first time in the emergency ward, but it was the first time I really thought I might lose her. She couldn't speak properly or see well. She couldn't feel her body and she had problems with her memory.

And she was terrified. It was heartbreaking to watch her little body shake. She kept asking if I could forgive her and that she did it for "a lot of reasons." The most painful part is that I knew exactly what she meant. Why she did what she did. Something beyond her ability to describe.

It's like a dark cloud that will not lift. And fear. Constant fear. Pressure on your chest. And loneliness. Knowing that if you screamed, nobody would hear you. That nobody would care. And you'd do anything to numb the pain. To just forget. And in a desperate search for relief, you want to hurt yourself.

That's why I started to run. And why I never liked answering the question, "Why do you run?" I ran because running hurt. My muscles ached and I couldn't breathe. Like an ice pick through my heart, it focused my mind on only trying to not collapse. The greater the physical pain, the deeper the emotional relief. It felt good to push until I could push no more.

My sisters and I have had lives of struggle. Ultimately, we just tried to survive. And sometimes it takes yet another brush with death to remember how many times running has saved my own life.

Out of all my sisters, Emma is the one who is most like me. I have to believe that she will find her way, just like I did. That we were both built to survive.

Emma still dabbles with drugs. And I still run. It's all I know how to do.

On Terry Fox

The Terry Fox Run was my first exposure to competitive running in middle school. Every September, the entire school participated in this event. I was a nerd back then, so for me it was an annoying inconvenience. But now that I'm a runner, the race has a different meaning.

Probably every Canadian knows the story of Terry Fox and his Marathon of Hope. In 1977, Terry Fox was diagnosed with osteosarcoma and had his right leg amputated. He was 19 years old.

After going through the medical system, Fox was both moved by the despair of those suffering from cancer and frustrated by the lack of awareness and money going into cancer research. He once said, "I'm sure we would have found a cure for cancer 20 years ago if we had really tried."

The night before his cancer surgery, Fox read an article about Dick Traum, the first amputee to complete the New York Marathon. That's when he knew that he wanted to run.

Fox wasn't always a runner. His true passion was basketball. In fact, the only reason he even began running in junior high was because his physical education teacher and basketball coach suggested that, due to his height, he might be better suited for long distance running instead of basketball.

Fox joined the cross-country team because he wanted to please his coach, but he never gave up on basketball. By the time he finished high school, he had a starting position on the basketball team and he won his high school's Athlete of the Year award.

After his amputation, Fox continued to play basketball in a wheelchair and went on to win three national titles. He was also named an All-Star by the North American Wheelchair Basketball Association in 1980.

Fox was not someone who liked to hear the word no, particularly about his athletic limitations. He believed in himself wholeheartedly. Fox ran his first marathon in British Columbia in 1979. He came in last place.

After that run, he revealed his plans for embarking on what he called the Marathon of Hope as a means to raise money for cancer research. His goal was to run across Canada and raise $1 for each of Canada's 24 million people.

The challenge that Fox set out for himself was brutal. He refused to take a day off and ran a marathon distance every single day with a leg prosthesis that forced him to limp and hop along slowly. He suffered blisters, shin splints, inflamed knees, tendonitis, cysts on his stump, and dizzy spells, among other obstacles. He refused regular medical checkups and suggestions that he was risking his future health.

He never made it across Canada. He was forced to stop when his cancer spread to his lungs and he could no longer breathe. He had hopes of recovering and finishing his run, but he passed away on June 28, 1981 at the age of 22. He had run for 143 days and covered 5,373 kilometers (3,339 miles).

Fox is a Canadian icon. After he passed away, the 15th Prime Minister of Canada, Pierre Elliot Trudeau, said of him:

"It occurs very rarely in the life of a nation that the courageous spirit of one person unites all people in the celebration of his life and in the mourning of his death … We do not think of him as one who was defeated by misfortune but as one who inspired us with the example of the triumph of the human spirit over adversity."

The *Toronto Star* was the first newspaper to regularly cover Terry Fox's run across Canada, assigning a reporter named Leslie Scrivener to follow him. Thirty years later, in April 2010, Scrivener wrote:

"It was so early that June morning. There was no hint of a sunrise when Terry Fox stepped on to Highway 17 in eastern Ontario. No one in the van with him had said a word. It was a time of waiting, of preparing. A long day, a marathon of running lay ahead. The moon bathed the fields in a silvery light. Alone, without the crowds who would later wait on the highway, he moved smoothly and contentedly through the dark. It was a good day, one of the rare ones.

The image from that morning endures, 30 years on. It's imprinted, somewhere, part of who I am.

In the three decades that have passed Canada too carries the imprint of the graceful young man with the awkward amputee's gait. He became a part of us, part of our bedrock. He is in our geography, in awards that honor outstanding young Canadians, as a role model for athletes."

Not all of us have a grand, life-changing purpose for running. But running changes you. And as Fox discovered — it makes you brave.

On Religion

My father was a Baptist minister. At Easter, he loved to play on the fact that in the Resurrection story, Mary goes to visit Jesus' tomb early in the morning while it was still dark. So our morning service started before the sunrise.

Only about half our congregation ever showed up, and those who did were always sleepy. For my family, it meant high stress and low energy. It felt like we were putting on a production, and it was hard for me to feel inspired. Something was missing.

I have been behind the scenes at church my entire life. I know the politics. I know the sermons. I know the language. I know all the hymns by heart.

And I think my dad chose to focus on the wrong detail of the resurrection story.

When Mary got up early, she didn't do it because she wanted to sacrifice sleep. She did it to be alone with someone she loved. She sought solitude.

And it was in that solitude that Christ spoke to her. Not behind concrete walls but under the shade of a tree. Not in a pew, but in a garden. One Easter, I wanted to be like Mary. I wanted to be alone.

I showered and got dressed with the same care and preparation that I normally would for church, except I put on running clothes. I waited for a time when all the local church services had begun. Then I started to run.

The route to my local cemetery took me through several residential streets. I passed three churches, but I was looking for a tomb. The cemetery is in a circular shape with an enormous cross on a huge pillar right in the middle of it. I ran toward the cross.

Everybody missed the very first Easter. They were sleeping. Or at church. Or going about their business. But Mary was right there. She knew where to look.

I love the part in the Bible that says that Mary ran home that day from the tomb. After she told the disciples, they ran back to the tomb. It says that one disciple even outran the other and arrived first.

Easter is not a day for sitting. It's a day for running.

I take comfort in knowing that it doesn't matter how far or how fast I run, whether I'm in church or pushing a sprint. Every Easter morning, Christ will roll that stone away to find me.

Chapter 2:
Finding Myself & Discovering Trails

On Destiny

My name, Vanessa, means "butterfly". And I share a connection with these fascinating creatures. Growing up, I felt awkward and uncomfortable in my own skin. I felt lumpy and hairy and ugly, like a caterpillar.

Running on trails transformed my body and my ambitions. The metamorphosis allowed me to take flight. And the more I grew into my own skin, the more I had in common with the butterfly.

The monarch butterfly embarks on a pilgrimage of 2,000 miles every year, a distance I can run on an annual basis. It flies from Canada to Southern California, fluttering as far as Mexico. This parallels my own move from Toronto to San Diego, and my cross into the Mexican border to secure a work visa.

In ancient times, the monarch was called "the wanderer," a nickname I can relate to as a nomad. While exhibiting both strength and resilience, the butterfly remains delicate. Its colors, while beautiful to us, are actually colors of fierce warning to their predators.

This reminds me of a trick that endurance runners sometimes pull in the overnight stages of an ultra, particularly during 100-milers. When they are closing in on their competition overnight, they turn off their headlamps. The darkness provides them cover, and by the time they are right on top of their target, it is too late. They pass their competitors easily.

I compare this with my own tendency to wear bright colors on the trail and light up the path as much as I can. At my last 100, I carried three handheld flashlights, on top of one headlamp. I'm not usually fast enough to pass people overnight, but even if I could, I'm not sure I would turn off my lights. Let them see me coming. My colors are their warning.

Monarch butterflies leave no trace of their presence. They eat their own chrysalis and their residues after birth, so no one will know they were ever there. I compare this to my own drive to leave my natural outdoor environment as untouched as possible.

Sadly, the beautiful monarchs that begin the journey south are not the same ones who finish it. Along the way, they die. Their descendants take up the torch and continue the journey. Someday, I too will pass. I hope that I will expire on a journey to a beautiful place, leaving a destination for others to follow.

When I spot a butterfly on the trail, I take it as a sign that I'm exactly where I am supposed to be. In the book, *What I Talk About When I Talk About Running*, Haruki Murakami writes: "A person doesn't become a runner because someone recommends it. People basically become runners because they're meant to."

I think a lot about what I'm meant to do. I realized when I left my office job that I was spending too little time doing what I loved. Not enough running. Not enough writing.

Running for me is a lifelong pursuit, and that's not something that everyone will understand. People may accuse me of having an addiction, not finding enough balance in life, or neglecting day-to-day responsibilities. I've learned that instead of trying to explain myself, it's best to leave my running unjustified. I am happy. And I don't need to make apologies for the lifestyle I've chosen.

You don't have to be a runner to hear similar accusations. Whenever we make a positive change in our lives, there will always be accusers and de-motivators. Sometimes these people are very close to us. I shook them off and surrounded myself with supporters instead.

I echo Murakami when he says:

"I'm going to keep running... and not let it get me down. Even when I grow old and feeble, when people warn me it's about time to throw in the towel, I won't care. As long as my body allows, I'll keep on putting in as much effort—perhaps even more effort—toward my goal of finishing... I don't care what others say—that's just my nature, the way I am. Like scorpions sting, cicadas cling to trees, salmon swim upstream to where they were born, and wild ducks mate for life."

I am a monarch. I was born to fly on the trails, and that's where you'll find me.

On Trail Running

One Tuesday, after I had settled into a new journalism job in San Diego, I decided to try an organized lunchtime trail run with some co-workers. I didn't know anyone, so I was eager to meet some fellow trail junkies. I had been hanging around ultrarunners for several weeks, and found a kinship with them that got me excited — for the first time in my introverted life — at the thought of meeting new people and making trail friends.

My office building overlooked a glorious canyon. In my mind, we would head to a secluded, scenic, and rugged single track trail. Instead, we ran around the parking lot, and then along a flat, dirt section, turned around, and came back. We never went into the canyon.

The group I was with was aiming for a negative split (running the second half faster than the first half). I was the only one without a watch and the only weirdo without shoes. I don't know what my splits were, but I know the canyon looked awesome and I missed out.

The leader said because I didn't have a watch, I should just try to stick with someone. So I thought I would keep pace with the girl in last place, and enjoy a good conversation. But she stuck in her headphones instead.

I have to accept that not everyone runs the way that I do. That doesn't make me better or worse — just different. Some people wear watches and keep track of their time. Not everybody stops when they see something interesting. Not everyone changes their pace to suit their dogs. And some people stick plugs into their ears so they can't hear interesting things.

I've seen articles that come up with cool lists about what type of runner you are. They give you a name and a description. It took me 30 years to figure out what type of runner I was. But at least now I can speak for myself:

I'm a trail runner. I don't always wear shoes, though I don't care in the least what others wear. I will always be attracted to the story of the person in last place. I'd rather be the last runner who saw a cool thing that everyone else missed, than to be a speedy runner who had a miserable experience. I don't particularly care about negative splits. I don't always know how far or how long I've run.

I like to run until I feel good. Then I like to keep running until I feel terrible. If there's a stream, I want to splash in it. If there's a tree, I want to climb it. I feel that people should look up more often and realize what a beautiful city San Diego is. And how amazingly lucky they are to run alongside a canyon at lunch.

I don't talk much during a run, but I hear everything. I'm not always the best conversationalist, but I do want someone around in case I spot something awesome, like a funny-looking bug.

Trail runners are incredible people. They'll literally take the shirt off their backs and give it to you. Or pour the last of their water into your bottle. They'll sit down with you if you need to sit. They'll run when you want to run. They don't care who you are, they'll look out for you.

Trail runners don't run around parking lots and come back. They carve their way deep into the canyons and gravitate towards each other there. Like magnets.

On San Diego

Someone once asked me how to find a city where you belong. The person felt out of place in the city they were in, but wasn't sure where they could feel at home. I suggested they determine their passions, and physically move to a location that was well known for that passion and where they could practice it full-time, year round. That's what I did when I moved to San Diego.

My passion was trail running, but the trail running community at the time was lacking in Toronto. I didn't own a car, so many well-known trails an hour's drive from my home were inaccessible to me. I was surrounded by tall buildings and a lively city nightlife I didn't love.

The weather made it difficult to run year-round, and the ultra community seemed non-existent. Toronto only had two marathons a year, while my San Diego friends seemed to race every weekend. It was always running weather in California.

When I moved, I had no Plan B. If it didn't work out, I had nothing to come back to. Still, I packed all my possessions into one carry-on bag, and took the flight. As soon as I landed, it suddenly didn't matter that I had no job and no money. I was home.

There's something about San Diego that gets me. The running here is something straight out of my dreams: hills, mountains, beaches, caves, and canyons. I feel so blessed and fulfilled running these trails.

In my first week, I was offered a steady job and a work visa. I even won Chargers game tickets. In seven short days, I had more running friends in San Diego than I ever had in Toronto. Everything fell into place.

On my trail runs, I would marvel at my surroundings and try to figure out how I got here. What did I do right to end up here? Had I taken a shortcut? Could I have gotten here sooner?

Running San Diego makes me feel closer to God, despite what people in Toronto prophesied. They said that I would stray far from God, that I would never find peace, that God would punish — not bless — me for the rest of my days.

I think those people I hurt needed to believe in divine justice. They need to think that God is avenging them. Yet here I bask in the feeling of running near Him. I bound through God's country, and on these lands I know Him better.

Perhaps God doesn't deal in rewards and punishments as much as we think, but instead teaches us daily what matters most: the rich, orange sand sifting through naked toes. And finding Him in our own backyard, regardless of where we call home.

On Love

All my life, I believed that love required hard work. It took the full effort and attention of two people to make a marriage work. Extreme commitment was needed to pull through the hard times, to overcome boredom, and to stay faithful. It was hard to keep any relationship alive.

It was with this mindset that I struggled through my first two relationships. I put up with a lot. I made compromises. I complained little. And every once in a while, I'd explode into a fit of tears and frustration. But it was all in a day's work, because love is hard.

Over time, my stress levels got higher and the more I gave, the more my partners would take from me. I felt parts of me start to wither and fade — essential parts of my personality. I felt burdened and taken for granted. But I was working hard to make my relationship work.

When I moved to San Diego and started dating Shacky, I learned a different perspective on love. We didn't have the couple "talks" and we didn't try to define anything. We just were. And it was easy. I never pushed him to do anything or be anything, and he returned the favor. We just took each other at face value, grateful for the company.

We never fought. We always made fun of each other. It was hard for me to imagine a relationship with playful waves, but no storms. Today, our lives are full of simple pleasures, and very few reasons to argue. We sit outside the RV, we play with the cat, and we run with the dog. There are no bills to quarrel over, and no responsibilities to divide. It's a dream-like existence.

Shacky and I do most things the opposite of traditional couples, and that fascinates me. None of the love songs make sense for us. We don't feel sick apart from each other, because we are each complete in ourselves. We don't feel that we can't live without the other; we'd just prefer not to.

We're free to come and go as we please — yet we please to stay close. We play on the same team, so there are no sides. Every favor done for the other is a favor done for ourselves. There are no egos and no battles. When one of us is strong, so is the other.

Love for me is neither gumdrops and rainbows, nor constant effort and hardships. Shacky and I have no extremes. We just exist in the same space.

I've learned that you can't invest your whole life into pleasing a person who is not yourself. And you can't sacrifice so much that you compromise doing what you love. When two people are happily travelling their own journey and just happen to be moving in the same direction — maybe that's love. Struggling and anxiously working to make a relationship work is perhaps not love at all, but wasted effort. Like running with your arms flailing and waving around. Just useless.

I'm no expert, but these are the thoughts I entertain about my own happy love life. Relationships are complicated, but I finally know what works for me. I need things simple and carefree. I need to be with my best friend, and our furry, four-legged kids, sleeping all on the same bed in a tiny RV, and running in the mountains. To me, that's love.

On Writing

My first day of journalism school, I was full of nerves. I had been accepted to one of the most reputable journalism programs in Canada, and the first thing on my schedule was a five-hour reporting class.

I walked into a room full of computers, not knowing what to expect. There were 30 other students there, and nobody knew each other. Within minutes, we had an assignment that was due right away.

We were told to choose someone in the room and describe them in such a way that they could be easily pictured—without mentioning any of their physical traits. We could instead make assumptions about their personality, their background, where they had been and where they were going. Essentially, we were to judge them.

The purpose of the exercise was to teach us to describe things accurately in a way that we were not accustomed to. To go beyond physical descriptions. Afterwards, we would do an icebreaker game to get to know each other and to see whether our judgments had been on target.

I was sitting in the corner so I had a great view of the room. I picked a girl who was sitting near the front. She was fair-skinned and tall with light brown hair. She was very pretty—long eyelashes and strong cheekbones. But I didn't write any of that down.

Instead, I wrote about how she had lived a life of privilege. Never worked hard a day in her life. I wrote about how supportive her parents were. How many friends she had had in high school. How she had always been popular. I wrote that she was ordinary. That her day-to-day life was boring. No depth. No complications. No surprises.

Then we all handed in our work.

Our teacher collected the papers and skimmed through them right in front of us. Then — to my horror — he started reading mine out loud.

There were no names involved — we didn't know each other's names and the teacher didn't reveal mine — so nobody knew who I had written about. But I slowly watched the girl at the front grow angrier and angrier. Her cheeks turned a bright red. Her lips tightened and with each sentence she grew more furious. Then she exploded.

She ranted about how this was not appropriate, how you can't judge people this way, how what I had written was obscene. I thought: This is it. I'm about to be expelled.

My teacher sat quietly, perched on his stool until the girl was finished. Then he calmly pointed out that the very fact she had recognized herself proved that I had done a great job. He said that a great writer will always draw strong emotions from the people who read his or her work, whether those feelings be positive or negative. Sometimes when people get upset, it's a good sign. We're pulling at their humanity and touching the rawness of their emotions.

At the end of our icebreaker, I understood why the girl had been so upset. At the very end of my piece I had written that someone like her could only have two possible names — I boldly predicted that she was either a Jennifer or a Sarah.

Her name was Sarah.

Since then, my writing has evoked many other strong emotional reactions, both positive and negative. Over time, this feedback gave me confidence in myself. I learned that when you are doing something right, people react. Strongly.

Earlier this year I wrote a blog that expressed my opinion on a Pearl Izumi ad campaign. I liked the ad campaign and thought it was clever. Others disagreed and found it (and the fact that I liked it) highly offensive.

I was surprised by the vindictive attacks and backlash it inspired. Two people even contacted my employer and tried to get me fired. You can still read the original post on my blog.

The incident helped me take a critical look at where I was going with my writing. I realized that I didn't want to write for my employer's audience. They were runners, but I had little in common with them.

I also started to realize that what I did want was to run trails for a really long time, and write this book.

On Safety

Every once in a while you hear a terrible news story about a woman who has been attacked or killed while on a run. For the weeks that follow, female bloggers write about safety and express anxiety about their own runs. One of the common questions I get is how I manage to stay safe on the trails.

I actually feel safer on a trail than a road, because there are fewer people around. A tree isn't going to jump up and rape me. I am more likely to be hurt by a snake or mountain lion on the trails that I run.

I'm not sure if it's from growing up in a rough area or from watching out for my sisters, but I have great spidey senses. I'm also smart enough to trust my sixth sense completely. The second I feel a slight discomfort, I split. Sometimes I don't even know if that discomfort is justified, or what to attribute it to. But I don't stay to find out. Ever.

When my spidey sense isn't going off, I am very bad at feeling fear. The things that most people are afraid of, I'm not. And I've always been that way. I'm insatiably curious and I always want to explore places I've never been. When faced with the unknown, I respond with excitement and eagerness instead of fear. I don't think about what may happen and I've been told that I can be reckless.

When I am faced with real danger, my instinctive reaction is anger. I get loud, strong, and aggressive. I never act like a victim—I'll fight back with everything I have.

Lastly, running with a dog goes a very long way as far as safety. Our pup Ginger is the sweetest dog, but I have no doubt that she will aggressively defend me if necessary. As far as wild animals, she can sense things that I cannot see. She keeps me on my toes, and is also a strong deterrent for potential attackers.

If you don't run with a dog, I cannot say enough about the benefits of doing so. My boyfriend and I volunteer as dog runners at the Humane Society. There are so many beautiful (and trained) animals there, capable of running alongside any human. Please consider adoption if you are looking for a dog to run with.

On Dogs

For as long as I can remember, the first and only thing I wanted consistently throughout my life was a dog. Growing up, I would daydream about having a pooch tag along at my heels while I went about my way.

One day, after my mom died, my dad came home with a little box. I opened it up and my heart stopped. Staring up at me were the big brown eyes of the most precious Lhasa Apso puppy I had ever seen. I had never felt so much joy in my little heart. I named him Cookie.

The thrill was so intense that I still compare any present and future pleasures to that one moment: if getting my puppy was 100, finishing an ultra is perhaps an 85. A great orgasm maybe a 90 to 95.

But in the months that followed, I struggled to understand why my dad bought that dog at all. We never put any food or water out for him, and we never took him outside to do his business. When he started pooping around the house, my dad angrily threw him into the laundry room.

We lived in government housing at the time, and the laundry room was a tiny cell-like structure about the size of a large closet, and detached from the house. We had to go outside and past the underground parking lot to get there. It smelled like urine and it was pitch dark.

I wasn't allowed to visit Cookie, but when my dad was out I would sneak away to see him. I loved him so much.

Food was scarce for all of us. We had a bottle of ketchup in the fridge and some limes, neither of which the dog would eat. My dad would eat out for his meals. Sometimes he would take us to the food court at the mall and buy us a meal, or before I went to school he would buy me a sub from 7-11 for lunch. But Cookie was hardly fed.

Over time, I watched my dog wither away. The sorrow of watching the light dim from his eyes squeezed my heart like a chokehold. Worse than my own hunger or neglect, it was a grief I had not yet known. Watching my puppy slowly die is a memory so engraved in my psyche that it still brings tears to my eyes.

One day, I went to visit Cookie and he was gone. My dad said he had run away, and to this day I don't know if that's true. He couldn't open the door alone, and I'm not sure he had the strength to escape. As I grew older and began to fully understand the extent of Cookie's abuse, I was afraid to ask my dad what had really happened. I daydreamed that he had run away and found a loving home, but in my heart I feared the worst—that my dad had "taken care" of him.

My dad went on to remarry and went to seminary. He graduated and became the minister of a small Spanish-speaking Baptist church. We moved out of government housing and into a small apartment, and there was food in our fridge again. Our lives normalized, and we were faithful church-goers.

In church, I was taught that God had given us dominion over all nature and animals, and that was why humans were the superior creation. Animals did not have souls, so we didn't have to worry about them. Our primary focus in life was to win souls for Christ, and any effort spent bettering the life of an animal was a wasted one. It was the same thing for love of nature or environmentally-focused ambitions. Our sights were on the eternal—we were only here for a short time. This world did not matter. It would be gone soon anyway.

I tried to believe these things. It would have been easier if Cookie had no soul. I wanted to believe that he didn't matter. But years later at the Born to Run 50K, I lost my last shred of faith in that possibility.

I ran the race with Ginger, a dog that my boyfriend Shacky had adopted as a puppy. She had been abandoned in Tijuana—a little mutt whose breed could not be identified. We think she might be a pointer but when people ask, we say she is Mexican.

Built long and lean, she was a tremendous runner and extremely passionate about the outdoors. I would often run her down to Penasquitos Canyon to a clear, cool waterfall where she could drink. We met an old man there once taking a hike with his wife. He pointed at the dog and said, "The thing about pointers is that they never grow up."

He was right. Ginger was nine years old, and all puppy. She still hopped and jumped and pounced and responded enthusiastically to the leash or a ball. We would run for more than twenty mountain miles, and after coming home she'd be eager to play some more. I could hardly keep up.

The Born to Run 50K was such a low-key trail race that Ginger ran the entire distance with me off-leash. I tried to do it barefoot, but had to stop after the first 10 miles due to rough, gravelly terrain. It took us a brutal seven hours to finish that first section but Ginger was my protector the entire time, looking up at me with patience and care.

On the next loops, my legs were exhausted. But Ginger pressed me on. She would run just in front of me, keeping a slow and steady pace and looking over her shoulder to make sure I was keeping up. If I slowed down, she nudged me forward. If I sped up, she pulled me back. When I was too tired to follow the course markings, she noted them and led me through all the right turns, correcting me a couple of times. I had never seen her like this.

Climbing up along the ridge, we ran through a glorious sunset and I fell into her steady, unwavering pace. It was like there was no one else on earth. Just two bitches on the trail. And I drew from her strength.

Even her face seemed to change. No longer puppy, she was the boss on this course. Responsible and caring. Watching out for my needs. She was running me.

I can't say whether or not dogs have souls but I do understand the spiritual connection that exists between a man and his beast. And I know from both growing up in the church and falling in love with dogs that being cruel to animals does not make you kinder to humans. That is a key flaw in the religious argument I was raised with.

In the Bible, Jesus speaks about small details of nature. He said that the eye of God is on the sparrow. God makes sure the sparrow has food to eat and beautiful feathers to clothe himself in. Does a sparrow need anything? God feeds him. How much more, Jesus asks, does God care for us? We are more than sparrows.

In other words, those who care for animals will care for humans even more. Those who are kind to nature are even kinder to mankind. I have sadly found the opposite to also be true: If you cannot feel compassion for a dog, how can you have compassion on your fellow human beings? If you do not feed your dog, you will not feed your children. If you neglect your animal, you will neglect your family.

Cruelty is just plain cruelty. To nature, to dogs, to children, to adults. You are just a cruel person. On the other hand, if you can love and sacrifice and care for an animal, it is unlikely you will turn away a human in need. And that has been my experience.

These days, Ginger's mileage matches my own. We train together. She keeps me focused on the trail and I keep her healthy and happy. And although Cookie's time with us was short and miserable, the pain of losing him is still raw in my heart. But I know that he left me a legacy. He taught me that it was okay to open my heart and feel a full affection for all living things.

If God's eye is on the sparrow, why isn't ours?

On Aging

When I was in nutrition school, I had a tightly packed schedule. I loved Wednesdays because that was the only day I could cross-train—pool swimming in the middle of the day like a retired senior citizen. In fact, that was my company when I swam—a pool full of my elders.

I love old people. The ones at my pool had it all figured out. They knew exactly what swimming was supposed to be like—easy and effortless, with a priority on social interaction. But that didn't mean they were not strong swimmers.

One of the most amazing things to me was to watch them transition from a slow, awkward gait on land to slipping into the water and immediately taking off—suddenly stronger and faster than me. Fishlike. They didn't breathe hard and always appeared to be taking their time, even though they were going twice my speed.

Sometimes the old guys would pause to smile and wave me ahead, as if I had a chance at staying in front. They assumed that because I was younger, I would be more impatient. And often I was.

Their vibe was calm and relaxed, as if they had the rest of eternity to finish their laps. Nobody looked at the clock. Nobody timed their breaks. So I learned to be more patient. And to appreciate everything my body can do.

In the change rooms, I was the hero. The only one with quick fingers and a strong grip, ideal for peeling and lifting and picking things up. Old wet skin is sticky and my help was often solicited in one form or another, usually to peel clothes off or pull them on. I would be rewarded with a warm smile and if I was lucky, a friendly pat.

Few words were exchanged because of a language barrier—these were Asian immigrants. But although they were old, they carried themselves with dignity and honor, as if their lives were just beginning and they still had one hundred more years to live. They smiled at me kindly but knowingly—as if I knew nothing and they knew it all. Maybe they were right.

Physically, it was another world. Have you ever seen a naked old lady? My first time was quite a shock. They look slightly inhuman, and gravity is suddenly a terrible thing. Important things get misplaced, or disappear completely. But the most jarring is the sudden realization that I might actually look like that someday.

These ladies didn't seem to care. Younger female swimmers cover up self-consciously, or hide in corners. They may try to sneak a peek at other women's bodies for comparison. But my afternoon ladies stood naked in the middle of the hall and yelled at each other from across the room, laughing and chattering the entire time. Clothes were an after-thought. They didn't look at bodies; they looked at faces. And they taught me a lot.

I learned to love my own skin and see more wonders than defects. To take my time and never rush. And to do my best to help others along the way.

On Hobbits

Hobbits are a diminutive race that inhabit the lands of Tolkien's Middle Earth. That is the Wikipedia definition. But they are much more than that.

Hobbits are silly little creatures and my childhood companions. They're an honorable race who taught me about life and adventure as I hid under my blankets with a flashlight, way past my bedtime. I love hobbits because reading about them running in their worlds inspired me to run in mine.

The Hobbit is my favorite book, and I anticipated the release of *The Hobbit* movie for years. I'm a nerd-turned-runner, and hobbits taught me pretty much everything I know.

I ran my first race in 2007, a clumsy 10K. Over the years since, I have built confidence, improved my mileage, and enhanced my cardio. I have read countless running books and articles and magazines. I have studied sports nutrition and completed ultramarathons.

But despite all I have learned about running, no lessons have been more valuable as the ones I picked up long ago from a plump little hobbit named Bilbo. I keep the following hobbit wisdom close to my heart:

1. Seek Adventure

"I am looking for someone to share in an adventure that I am arranging." - *The Hobbit*

Running is about a journey, not a destination. All the elements of life are compressed into this one activity. I can feel happy, sad, tired, excited, defeated, victorious, hungry, and hopeful all in the same journey. Running is an adventure. Seek it out.

2. Be Brave

"Hobbits are usually very shy creatures, but are nevertheless capable of great courage and amazing feats under the proper circumstances." - Wikipedia

I may not always look brave. Sometimes I look like an unlikely athlete—that's okay. Hobbits never look like warriors either. They're hairy and smelly and chunky. They hardly ever look strong or brave, and yet they are. So am I.

3. Always Keep Moving

"Go back? . . . No good at all! Go sideways? Impossible! Go forward? Only thing to do! On we go!" - Bilbo Baggins

Speed is overrated. Hobbits travel far and wide on their pudgy legs. They scale mountains and cross rivers. They see sights and breathe air in places where the fastest runners have never been. They can do this not because they are fast, but because they always keep moving.

4. Eat a Second Breakfast

Pippin: "What about breakfast?"

Aragorn: "You've already had it."

Pippin: "We've had one, yes. What about second breakfast?"

(Aragorn turns and walks off in disgust)

Merry: "I don't think he knows about second breakfast, Pip."

There is no reason to snub food when you are running many miles. Some of us struggle with eating just one breakfast. Hobbits eat two. That may be the secret to their remarkable endurance.

5. Love the Outdoors

"I want to see mountains." - Bilbo Baggins

Hobbits were born to be outdoors, and so were humans. We share an exploring nature and an affinity for climbing things and getting dirty. If you ever want to run with a hobbit, you're going to have to take it outside.

6. Always Have a Pocket

"What have I got in my pocket?" - Bilbo Baggins

Pockets are your most important running gear. You never know what shiny thing you may find under a rock, or how it might change your life.

7. Run Barefoot

"I have always enjoyed going barefoot and when I was growing up I seldom wore shoes, even when I went into town." - Zola Budd

Hobbit feet are rather large, covered with curly hair. Hobbits have leathery soles and hardly ever wear shoes. Hobbits are not embarrassed by their feet, and never notice if they get strange looks.

They love the feeling of rough or soft surfaces on their toes and they could spend all day pattering around barefoot. Humans are also capable of experiencing these pleasures.

8. Rely on Running

"The world is indeed full of peril and in it there are many dark places. But still there is much that is fair." - *The Lord of the Rings*

We live in an unstable world. Trends come and go so quickly that sometimes we want something ageless. Hobbits never change. Year after year, you can find them running through the same pages of your worn-out paperback. You can even throw them into your backpack and take them along on your next adventure. Running also never changes. The act of running is pure and timeless.

9. Age Means Nothing

"Hobbits really are amazing creatures. You can learn all there is to know about their ways in a month, and yet after a hundred years they can still surprise you." - Gandalf

A hobbit comes of age at 33. A 50-year-old hobbit is only barely entering middle age. Hobbits are not limited by their ages, and neither should we be.

10. Run With Your Heart

"I don't know if I could run 50 leagues over four days. I'm not Aragorn or Geoff Roes yet, but just perhaps I could be Frodo. Not quite a son of Numenor, but at least a hobbit." - Chris van Dyke, English teacher and ultrarunner

It is better to run with your heart, not your feet. That way even if you are slow, you can still feel everything.

On Books

When I was a child, my dad gave his books human names and referred to them as his "friends." We were not to disturb his books in any way. No folded pages. No food that might be spilled on them. No bending their spines.

After my dad's divorce, he left the country and left his books in my care. In the months that followed, I left the country, came back, and then moved around a lot. I didn't always have a home, but I always carried his books with me. They were heavy and burdensome—I was lugging around a library when I had almost no other possessions.

I reached a point where I could no longer store them. I had no place to live, and no place to put them. I also had no idea whether I was ever going to see my dad again. I didn't know where he was, had no way of contacting him, and he had been gone for a long time. So I gave them away.

I continued working and moving around until I was finally able to rent an apartment and support myself. I went back to school. That's when my dad showed up, asking for his books. When I told him I had given them away, he was upset.

He made such an issue of it that the person who owned the books gave them back to avoid a confrontation. With his books in tow, my dad disappeared again. And I never looked at books the same way again.

Today when I pick up a book, I see a person. A writer who bore a part of his or her soul in an effort to benefit others. I see hours of his time, the agony of over-thinking every phrase, and the burden of creating something fresh and meaningful. A book is a part of them reaching out to me.

Malcolm Gladwell's book *The Outliers* was one publication I identified with. This isn't a book about running, but about success. Gladwell describes in detail what it takes to become successful, rich, or famous. And it's not what you think.

Gladwell defines "outliers" as "something that is situated away from or classed differently from the main or related body." An outlier is a special person, unlike the rest of us. The very smart. The very wealthy. The very successful. Gladwell tells us what it takes to get there.

At the end of the book, Gladwell speaks openly about his personal history and the legacy from which he has come. He speaks of what his mother and grandmother did in order to give him the opportunities that made him successful, and he credits much of his rise as a writer to the legacy these women built for him.

I don't have this. It isn't something I can fake or change. But in response to Gladwell's thoughts about legacy, in 2010, I wrote the following in a margin:

This is what I want to do for my children. I think about it all the time. About what kind of legacy and opportunities I can give them.

I feel like I understand my link in the generational chain of greatness. I am the one with the rough past. The one that changed the direction of her family tree – from nobodies to somebodies. All my time and efforts have been focused on making this switch. I am the grandmother and the mother who will someday be highly praised, but I will not personally ever be famous or rise to great power.

I was not given the gift of opportunity from my parents. But my children will have it. As will their children. And among them – there will be outliers.

In 2011, I ran my first ultra. Then I ran more. Then I won first place in my age group. And I ran my first sub-6 hour 50K. Suddenly I began to re-think that note in the margin.

What if I could be an outlier? All those opportunities I thought would be for my children – why couldn't I seize them for myself? Why couldn't I step out from behind the shadows and grasp my own dreams?

So what if I didn't have a legacy behind me. So what if I didn't have the right history. And then I realized I wasn't even sure I wanted children. Even if all I do is run in the mountains with my boyfriend and my dog until I die there, I want to forge my own path. I want to seize my own happiness.

On Vanity

When I was 13, my dad said that if I shaved my legs I'd turn into a whore and God would be displeased. But as a hairy pubescent pre-teen, *I* was displeased. I felt like Wolverine. Very fuzzy.

Every summer, I tried to wear pants for as long as possible. When it got too hot, I would shamefully wear shorts. I was already socially awkward, so my hairy legs just further confirmed my status as a weirdo. I went to a posh high school where all the girls in my gym class were well-groomed mini-me versions of their upscale, manicured mothers. I already knew I had no chance of impressing them, so all I wanted was to not stand out too sorely.

Every day I begged my dad to let me shave. And every day my pleading fell on deaf ears. Then suddenly one day I annoyed him enough that he said yes—but under one condition.

I would only be allowed to shave ONE strip up the middle of my leg. One razor strip and nothing else around it. My dad's explanation was that this would show me how horrible shaving was. He told me that one strip would grow back stubble so thick and so black that I would never want to shave again.

In retrospect, I struggle to understand what I was thinking when I agreed to this. Maybe I was just excited by the fact that he said yes in some way. Or maybe I didn't really believe he would let me walk around like that.

But for whatever reason—I grabbed the razor and shaved one strip straight up my leg at the very front from my ankle to my knee. Immediately afterwards my dad took the razor away and it suddenly dawned on me: I might as well be dead.

I had gym at school the next day and I had to wear shorts and play baseball. I realized that day that there IS actually something worse than a hairy pair of legs — a hairy pair of legs with two hairless strips...

I wanted to crawl into a hole and set myself on fire.

It was so beyond humiliating that nobody even made fun of me. It was way beyond that. People kind of looked at me, and I think they were scared. Only someone who was mentally deficient would do this to their own legs.

I walked around this way for a couple of days, until I had enough. I braced myself for the worst punishment of my life, and took a razor to the rest of my legs.

My dad didn't even notice.

In my teenaged years, my dad tried very hard to liberate me from any shred of teenaged vanity. I wasn't allowed to wear makeup or do my nails. I couldn't wear anything that didn't cover my knees. Our clothes, instead of coming from a store, came from huge black garbage bags that may or may not have been lifted from a Goodwill donation bin. They mostly contained old lady or old man clothes. And that was my wardrobe.

My dad's rules were extreme, but I wonder if they didn't work in some sick way, because after the half-leg-shave incident, I never felt ugly again. It's like he desensitized all my self-consciousness. Or I knew I'd never feel more ugly than I had with the freak legs. I had seen the worst of social stigma, and I never again worried about looking right to please a crowd.

Years later, coming home from the Nanny Goat 24 Hour Race, I unloaded the car and headed into the bathroom. I had been camping, and this was my first time using a real bathroom in days.

I caught a glimpse of my own reflection and it surprised me. I realized that I had just spent three days without looking in a mirror. Not even thinking, or missing the absence of my own reflection.

I stood in the bathroom and took a deep look. My skin was darker than I remembered. I had a new tan. My eyes were bright and shining, and my cheeks were rosy. My hair was still in messy pigtails, looking playful but not out of place. Most importantly, I had a huge smile on my face.

This is my ultrarunning look.

As more miles passed under my feet, I also trampled my insecurities one by one. I replaced my long dark hair with thick, tangled dreads and learned to let go. It was the details that made all the difference: no longer checking my reflection when I passed car windows. No longer smoothing out my hair before a photo was taken. And to my surprise, I looked better when I wasn't trying.

In nature, we see beauty in randomness: twirling leaves and jagged rocks. Symmetry in the woods implies a human presence: when rocks are neatly stacked or when sticks are lined up. So why do we insist on symmetry to define our own beauty? Our imperfections say far more about our individuality and personal value.

Listening to nature as I run by, it seems to whisper:

"Let me layer you with leaves and sun. Let my mud design your tattoos, and let my waterfalls moisturize your skin. Breathe deep, relax, and trust me. I will make you beautiful."

On Elitism

When I first picked up Scott Jurek's book *Eat & Run*, more than anything I hoped his words would help me understand what sets an elite runner apart from the rest of us. What qualities do they have that we don't? What kind of drive, talent, training, or motivation pushes them to excel? Apart from raw running talent, can this be learned?

And most importantly, could I run better?

At San Diego 100 in 2012, I paced Jay Danek who finished well under 24 hours. Jay had previously finished his first 100 miler in an impressive 19 hours. Although Jay isn't an elite, watching him power uphill at around mile 80 changed my mind about running.

I was struggling to keep up with him, even though he had run 80 miles that day and I had run zero. I decided that I should start demanding more of myself. That I would start racing ultras, not just entering to finish. My main competition would be me. My drive was not to win races, but to run better than I previously had. I could do more. I could train.

Then I read *The New Yorker* magazine article by Malcolm Gladwell titled *Slackers: Alberto Salazar and the Art of Exhaustion*. Salazar was "the greatest distance runner in the world" for the first half of the 1980s. Gladwell's article shines a revealing light on Salazar's development as a person and a runner; I was surprised to see some commonalities with Scott Jurek's own accounts in *Eat & Run*.

The resounding theme was an acceptance of pain. Not just expecting, but embracing it. Letting it drive you. Running despite it.

With a background of barefoot and minimalist running, I was taught over and over again that pain was bad. "Running is not supposed to hurt," I was told. "If it hurts, you're doing it wrong."

While this may be true as far as perfecting your form, it appeared to me that there was a pain threshold somewhere that most people dared not cross. But those who did became elites. Elites had a willingness to push beyond what they were capable of accomplishing pain-free. And that's where they found greatness.

I don't think running is supposed to hurt all the time. But if running never hurts, I wonder if you're "doing it right." I wonder if you're growing or exploring your limits.

Since I started running in 2007, I have not had a single injury. I am reluctant to state that fact, unsure whether it's a good or a bad thing. Running is a sport plagued with injury. Does my non-injury reflect the fact that I'm not trying hard enough?

A few months ago I went on a group training run, followed by food and drinks. In the running conversation that ensued, someone suggested that running talent comes in many different forms. For some it was speed. For others, endurance. And for others, the ability to not get injured.

My ears perked up. Could my talent be an injury-free running career? I hoped so.

Coming home from San Diego 100, I decided to step it up. I cut down on my races and concentrated on training for specific 100-milers. I planned my runs. I incorporated speed training. I got help from a coach.

Where I had been running 12-minute miles, averaging around 30-mile weeks, I improved to running nine-minute miles, averaging 50-mile weeks. I'm still improving.

I had many firsts. Like hitting a 4:45 min/mile pace for the first time (only for about two seconds!) and running up a mountain so hard that I had to puke twice near the top.

While I want to run better, I'm not aiming to be an elite. I simply want to explore my potential, get lost in the mountains, and not be afraid of anything. Not even pain.

Sometimes our conception is that elites run effortlessly. We think they can cover a marathon distance and feel fresh, like they just started. But it seems the opposite may be true: Elites are willing to hurt more than anyone else. At the end of the Gladwell article, Salazar holds his hand over an open flame and says, "I feel that just as much as anyone else." But they are elites because they are not afraid of pain. Today, I try to remember that when I run.

On Race

I should have been born white. The first man to imply it was my dad. Then years later, my (now ex) husband would say it. And my partner after that. A unanimous verdict from the first three men in my life, all of them Hispanic. And I believed them.

To them, I wasn't submissive enough to be Hispanic. I had the gall of a white woman to question the men in my life. The nerve to dream about a life outside the kitchen. All indecent qualities in a woman, and hugely contributing to the breakdown of the family in North American culture.

I was born in El Salvador, but moved to Canada when I was three years old. So I was "raised white." Spanish was my first language and we spoke it at home, but I went through the Canadian school system and only made Canadian friends.

The men in my life used "white" as an insult. I remember my dad taking me out for meals and talking at length about why white women were not REAL women. Why they could never please a man. Why they were so cold and so wrong.

But Hispanic women were beautiful. They were gentle and kind and always did what they were told. They served others and they had kids. Lots of them.

They cooked and were happy with very little. They never wanted anything more than what they had, never asked any questions, and never did anything without permission.

The Hispanic women I knew all fit this mold. They could take abuse like "real women," be it verbal, physical, or emotional. As I understood, that's what made them beautiful. That's what men wanted.

My ex's mother was the epitome of the perfect Hispanic housewife. She is still a very pleasant woman—soft-spoken, attentive, and loving. But she had a bit of a darker side she suppressed that I found equally wonderful.

Secretly, she had a sharp wit, a bright mind, and a subtle passive-aggressiveness. When she first found out I was with her son, she got up in my face and scared the crap out of me. This quiet and humble woman, driven to rage. Though the moment itself was unpleasant, I later looked back on it as a rare glimpse into a very real place for her, and I admired her outburst.

Then there was the time she shut off the water in the entire apartment building to win a fight with a bitchy, loud-mouthed woman over a laundry room washing machine. My ex's mother didn't have the words or mannerisms to compete in a yelling match, so she quietly broke into the water control room instead.

After the enemy removed her hopelessly drenched clothes mid-wash, wondering what had happened to the water, my ex's mother turned the system back on and calmly started her own load. She giggled to tell the story, embarrassed by her actions. But it was little outbursts like these that made her awesome.

She didn't drive. Highly dependent on her husband, she was his faithful shotgun every time. She couldn't drive to the grocery store without him. But when we got a car racing video game, she cleared every sharp corner with stunning accuracy at blazing speeds, while her husband crashed into walls and couldn't compose himself.

She was a fighter, and I admired her. After I broke up with my ex, I knew I would never see her again. I would be afraid to cross her anyway. But knowing there are women like her out there — who can't quite be themselves all the time, but would make this world more interesting if they were — gives me the courage to be myself all the time.

To not be afraid of a sharp wit, an angry rant, or a sense of stubbornness. To have and exploit the full benefits of my imagination. My ambition. A desire for something better. My own voice. To not let anyone suppress me.

When I announced my decision to move to San Diego, I was told my decision was a "white" one. I was accused of thinking I was too good for my Hispanic crowd. The funny thing is, since moving to San Diego, I feel more ethnic than I did in Canada. Shacky jokes about my "Mexican" heritage and I eat way more Hispanic food here.

Running these mountains, it seems I've spent most of my life feeling homesick for a place I've never been. A place like this. Miles away from brown or white or black or yellow. A place where I can just be myself. Strong and determined. Maybe even a little crazy. Where the only colors that matter are the course markings I'm following to the finish line.

On Emotions

In the book *Born to Run*, Christopher McDougall wonders how our most primal impulses—fear and pleasure—play a role in our desire to run. He writes that as far as stress relief and sensual pleasure are concerned, running is just as relevant as sex.

I love this passage:

We run when we're scared, we run when we're ecstatic, we run away from our problems and we run around for a good time.

And when things look worst, we run the most. Three times, America has seen distance-running skyrocket, and it's always in the midst of a national crisis. The first boom came during the Great Depression, when more than two hundred runners set the trend by racing forty miles a day across the country in the Great American Footrace.

Running then went dormant, only to catch fire again in the early 70s, when we were struggling to recover from Vietnam, the Cold War, race riots, a criminal president, and the murders of three beloved leaders.

And the third distance boom? One year after the September 11 attacks, trail-running suddenly became the fastest-growing outdoor sport in the country. Maybe it was a coincidence. Or maybe there's a trigger in the human psyche, a coded response that activates our first and greatest survival skill when we see the raptors approaching us.

Running for me was born in the midst of personal turmoil during the worst stages of my life. But whenever I ask other people why they run, the answers are often something like weight loss or good health or love of the sport. So I thought I was alone in embracing running for its therapeutic effects. For me, running heals things that would otherwise be broken. But I never heard it described that way before reading *Born to Run*.

I was already running barefoot when this book came out, and already interested in ultras. But the book made me think about the primal links to fear and pleasure, and I tried to trace the role of some of my strongest human emotions in fueling my runs: fear, anger, and hope.

FEAR

When I started running, I lived in downtown Toronto—the shady side. My area was buzzing with people at all hours of the day and night, and there were areas that I ran through where I literally could not stop for fear of being attacked. Being followed was not uncommon.

But I was stubborn and ran anyway, propelled by an even greater fear: what my world would look like if I couldn't run.

I had a few close calls. I quickly learned to eliminate walking intervals. People would approach me if I was walking, but nobody would run after me. Running was the only way I could cross some of the most dangerous parts of town.

I could run right through a group of people that I would never dare walk past. If I ran fast enough, they would only stare. Once I jogged slowly and I got followed almost to my door. You better believe that I learned to run faster.

A few times I hoped a fence and snuck into a track at a local high school. People couldn't figure out how to get in, so they would stand at the fence and watch me like a cat watches a mouse in a cage. But I felt safe there. I would run circles around the track, propelled by the fear of the eyes on me, yet strangely finding peace in the midst of it.

Before I lived downtown, I lived in a west-side neighborhood, equally dangerous. Sometimes I could hear people screaming, getting beaten to near-death right outside my window in the middle of the night. But at the time my options were to either live there or live on the street.

My solution? I would grab my bike and ride it to the lake before dawn. To the trails I would eventually run. I would find peace there. Fear is what drove me there, and fear is what moved my legs. If it weren't for fear, I would not be a runner today.

ANGER

As I started gaining strength from running, my fears hardened into anger. I felt rage towards the people and events in my past. I was angry I had been oppressed, dismissed, abused, and abandoned. I listed to angry music on my iPod, and felt my blood boil as I ran. I used the anger as fuel and it made me faster.

HOPE

Over time, the anger started to soften. I felt strong and powerful instead of weak and vulnerable. I wasn't a victim anymore. Near the end of my runs, I felt a strong sensation of hope. I realized that everyone goes through personal struggles. I was hardly alone.

When we first take up running, it's tough. Our bodies and minds are challenged, and there's an element of suffering there. But suffering is not something new to us. We know how to suffer. And we also know how to stand.

Think of a life challenge that you may have overcome. A rough past. A shameful childhood. A dark secret. We are survivors.

We know how to endure. How to stand at a start line with senseless, irrational dreams. How to hope for not just a finish, but a win. With no track record or hope in hell... but somehow still believe that we just might.

We know how to grow wings on a barren trail. Turn noes into maybes. And maybes into yes.

Definitely yes.

And so we keep running.

On Extra Weight

It was just two weightless paper bills thrown in my direction, but they felt like a thousand pounds on my shoulders. I grabbed the forty dollars and stuffed them in my wallet. I felt heavy and exhausted.

I thought a healthy relationship was supposed to be a partnership, but ever since my then-boyfriend's brain injury, I was carrying all the weight.

I had met Danny back when I was a teenager. My dad was the pastor of a small Spanish-speaking congregation that Danny and his family attended. Since we were the only two young people there, we soon became close friends.

He was likable, social, and loved to make people laugh. I was quiet and withdrawn, but we were inseparable. Our church-based social activities were the same, and he was the only boy I was allowed to hang out with.

When a family from Argentina came to Canada and joined our church, he started dating their daughter, and I dated their son. Eventually, Danny married their daughter, and I married the son. When the family was deported, Danny's wife went back to Argentina. I moved to Argentina to live with my new husband, while Danny stayed in Canada.

Argentina and marriage weren't what I expected. I had no freedom, no life, and no future. I hated every second of it, and only lasted there for three months. I knew that divorce would carry a huge social stigma, so I didn't tell anyone I was coming home. Except Danny.

My social world collapsed after I left my husband. The only world I knew was the church, and they turned on me with an ugly ferocity that left me dumbfounded. Danny decided to leave his wife as well and we moved in together. The backlash from our families was so extreme that he moved back with his parents to try to smooth things over, but we kept seeing each other. That was when Danny had his accident.

As an electrician, Danny was changing a street light when the bucket truck underneath him started to move. He hit his head and knocked himself unconscious, dropping twenty feet to the pavement below. He landed on his head, and the bucket he was standing on fell on top of him. He was taken to the hospital in a coma and his case was later featured on the Discovery Channel as a miracle story.

The verdict from my religious world was unanimous: this was God's punishment for our infidelity and divorces, and his accident was my fault. His family nicknamed me "the witch" and refused to let me see him. So I just sat in the hospital hallway and cried.

Danny's recovery took well over a year, during which time I spent every spare moment in the hospital. I dropped out of school and went back to work to help with the bills. But the relationship with both our families was still shattered.

When Danny got a financial settlement for his accident, we bought a condo and moved in together. He continued to recover, but there were some changes that were permanent. Danny's frontal lobe had been damaged. His therapist explained that this was the center of motivation, drive, and inhibition. There was no way of knowing whether his personality would be changed.

I noticed the changes right away. The sudden burst of anger where he'd yell at me for the most random, insignificant things. A misplaced object. If I "forgot" something he swore he told me, but never did. I found myself walking on eggshells. His mood swings were unpredictable, but to the outside world he was calm and composed.

Danny couldn't go back to his old job due to psychological trauma, and he quickly became frustrated with his other options. He dropped out of school, and he didn't want to work at a job that was "beneath him." His experience as an electrician was useless. Forced to start over, he was overwhelmed by the enormousness of what he had lost.

While he floundered, I struggled to support us both. I was in nutrition school and we were getting some money from his settlement, but that would not last forever. When it ran out, I knew we'd be in trouble.

I opened my own nutrition practice, and worked another retail job on the side. Danny would spend his days at his parent's home, or surfing the web. All my pleading for him to get a job—any job—fell on deaf ears. I started eating into my credit to support us, and I knew I was headed straight for financial disaster.

I wanted so badly to be strong enough to carry us both. It wasn't even about him. I just wanted to be strong. Stronger than anyone else I knew. I told myself I had the drive and energy to carry those weights. Both mine and his. But my knees buckled under the extreme pressure.

Sometimes I wished he would just be a man, get over his drama, and get his ass working again. What kind of a man allows a woman to kill herself providing for them both, when he was able-bodied enough to contribute?

But I knew it wasn't that simple. I felt his brain injury had changed him. He had no drive. No motivation. It blew my mind because Danny used to be such a hard worker. Now he didn't seem to have anything left.

Every once in a while, when I lost my temper, he'd go out and do an odd job for a friend. He'd come home with $40 and toss it at me. I'd pick it up, but we both knew it was not enough. It was never enough.

My runs to and from work were my escape, but I still felt like I was running with an anvil chained to my ankle. I was burdened with many worries and too many bills. I had such a heavy heart.

The retail job I worked was one of those jobs where you stand around all day just to kill time, counting the hours and minutes before you can clock out. I'd get out late, run home, and collapse into bed. Then I'd get up the next morning for my nutrition practice. Wherever I went, I carried that anvil.

I started daydreaming what it would be like if I only had my own weight to carry. Only my own bills to pay and my own food to shop for. Everything that weighed me down could be cut in half. I would be light as a feather. I could actually move forward in my career. I'd have time to start writing a book. I could run the races I dreamed of. I could explore new trails.

My very first race was a 10K, but I showed up with enough hydration in my belt to last me for 50K. It was heavy to carry, but it made me feel safer having all that water and nutrition. I now carry less for 100 miles than I did for that first 10K. Not because I drink less, but because I'm less afraid.

Believing that things could be different was a challenge. The weights of my life, though heavy, were familiar. I worried that without them I wouldn't know how to function.

Still, I took the chance and left my brain-injured partner. Some could blame me, but others would not. I don't know if it was right or wrong to leave the way I did, but I know it was right for me. I was ready to unclip that anvil. I wasn't afraid anymore.

I found that by shedding those weights, I could indeed shake the dust off my wings. I could leave those bills on the dining room table and fly away to better things.

On My Parents

My stepmother was my first glimpse into a normal life. A world where not everything was from the devil. She listened to secular music. She painted her nails. She did her hair. She was happy and bubbly and very active in her church.

My parents met when she was organizing a sleepover at her house for the church pre-teen girls, and invited me to come. I had never been to a sleepover in my life; they were strictly forbidden. But she assured my dad that she would be the responsible adult in charge.

I vividly remember going through my stepmom's CD collection, enthralled at the variety of music. I loved music, but all we owned were Larnelle Harris and Sandy Patti cassette tapes, and I had already memorized them. My stepmom had Barenaked Ladies. I had never heard of them, and the name shocked me. I thought it was some sort of porn. When I put them on, I loved the sound. It was nothing like the stuff I had grown up with. She also had Amy Grant and the Gypsy Kings. I thought I was in heaven.

From my stepmom, I learned to love new adventures and to travel. To open my mind to new possibilities and to never be afraid to meet new people. She would tell us stories about her vacation in Ecuador, how she went fishing for piranhas, and even tasted one.

The idea of a woman traveling alone on such a trip was foreign to me, and I was mesmerized by her carefree spirit. She wasn't "in her place," as I had understood a woman's place to be, and she gave me courage to step out of mine.

But of most value to me was my stepmother's belief in my writing. As soon as she met me, she began to foster it. I was thirteen years old when I met her, and had no idea I was good at anything. She encouraged me to enter a writing contest for the city's paper *The Toronto Star*, and I won with a memoir I wrote about my first experience on a roller coaster.

I was asked to read my story aloud at Toronto's annual literacy fair, Word on the Street. There, I met my very first journalists, the editors of the *Star* who had judged the contest. They pressed on me the importance of continuing with my writing, and I said I would keep it up.

One of them approached my stepmom, shook her hand, and urged her, "Do not let your daughter stop writing." She said she wouldn't. Despite the many turbulent years that would follow, my stepmom kept her promise. And although my faith in her would sometimes waiver, she never once lost faith in me.

As the years passed, my relationship with my stepmom grew shaky. Not because of anything she did, but because of talks with my dad that changed my perspective. My dad would take me out for a meal, and explain why my stepmom could not be trusted. He would describe all the things that were wrong with her and why I should never be like her. He spoke very calmly and authoritatively, so I believed him. I really just wanted to spend time with my dad, and was silly enough to think that's what he wanted too. My stepmom had no idea we were having these talks.

It was only when I reached adulthood that I was able to see things clearly. My parents were struggling in their marriage, and my dad was desperately trying to keep his daughters on his side. While some parents go out of their way to shield their children from the strain of divorce, in our case, my dad drew lines in the sand and forced us to choose who we loved, as well as prove our loyalty.

The ultimate test of loyalty was when my dad used my name and ID to open a bank account that couldn't be traced back to him. He deposited money there that he had stolen from my stepmom, and swore me to secrecy.

I've often wondered what it was that pushed my dad off the edge to a controlling place. Some family friends have suspected mental illness, an accusation that enrages my dad. When you meet him, he is a perfect gentleman. He is calm, peaceful, and seems to exude humility. Never overly emotional, he inspires trust. He has a good sense of humor and kids love him. He was my first hero.

I share a lot of the same qualities as my father. We both have a biting wit, a silly sense of humor, and we're both the quiet and pensive type. We're both voracious readers. My dad is a thinker not a fighter, but he fights with words and influence. We have both been accused of having questionable morals.

My dad once told me that I was the only woman in his life who has been with him through everything, and I'm the only one who truly knew him. I believe that's true, but it's not a burden I'm proud to carry. I would rather still see him through rose-colored glasses, as my childhood hero.

Compared to his own childhood, my dad was an ideal father. I complain about neglect, but as one of more than 20 brothers and sisters, he was completely ignored and left to fend for himself. He knew neglect on a far deeper level.

My dad would steal food from pig troughs to get by, and was regularly beaten viciously by his grandmother. His own father was an alcoholic, and the abuse my dad knew, I never did. My dad wanted to be better than his parents. And he loved my birth mom with all his heart. Of that much, I am sure, because after she died he was never the same.

I get my mental toughness from my dad. When it came to exercise or physical labor, he never treated me like a kid. There were no exceptions or allowances — I had to keep up, or get left behind.

For years, my dad had a job as a janitor and he took me to work with him. We would clean offices, factories, and churches. I had my areas that I was responsible for cleaning, and the standards were high. I remember sweeping dusty factory floors, vacuuming office spaces, and scrubbing church toilets. The floors and the toilets were often my job. My dad said that no matter how smart we were, we must always be humble enough to scrub a toilet. I learned a suck-it-up attitude from these jobs, as complaining was never tolerated.

Today, I apply this mindset with running. There is no whining in running. If the aid stations suck, I am hardly above filling my own bottle. I am not too good to stop and help a fellow runner. And no matter how much I am hurting, I think twice before opening my mouth to complain.

Vanessa Runs

Chapter 3:
Traveling Far & Running Ultras

On Ultrarunning

When I was a kid, my English teacher called me to the front of the class after some province-wide standardized testing to tell me that my writing skills had scored at a grade 12 level.

I was in seventh grade.

That was the day I realized I was good at writing. I always knew that I liked it, but I didn't know I was any better at it than others. It was more than just practice or paying attention in class. I could see and express things in unique ways. I could inspire change.

That realization transformed my future. It defined my profession, the way I express myself, and who I am. When I ran my first trail ultra marathon at Noble Canyon 50K, I experienced a similar awakening.

Starting the race, I felt very inexperienced, so I took a spot near the back of the pack. My training had been great and the race began with a downhill section. I got caught behind several very cautious downhill runners, but I wasn't sure how to pass them on the single track. I got to the bottom of the canyon feeling like I had barely run at all.

Coming back up the canyon, the crowd was more spread out and I was running strong. Whenever I caught up to someone on the trail, I would slow down and size them up. If they looked fitter than me, I would stay behind them and assume they were better runners.

I started walking some inclines, not because I felt I needed to, but because the people in front of me were walking and I didn't feel I was experienced enough to pass them. I did this until I grew frustrated, and then it dawned on me: maybe I'm better than I realize. Did I have low runner's esteem? This is something I love, and it fits. Like writing.

Since then, I have had my fair share of races where I've felt much worse, but the joy of being on a trail is still there. A peaceful and appreciative awe of my beautiful surroundings.

When I'm on a trail, nothing feels foreign. I belong there. My body was built to move this way, and I can't help smiling and feeling at home. Different people have different talents, so I'm not particularly special. But I think that ultra distance trail running might be something I could develop. Something a little bit bigger than me.

A few months before, I had run a 60K mileage at my first timed race and raced a marathon the next day. After that, I felt like I could do anything. It gave me the courage to pursue a life I really wanted.

But this race did something else. This race made me feel like an ultra distance trail runner. It gave me the courage to pass people. It gave me a place on these trails. At the finish line, I could stand in the company of some amazing athletes and not feel like just a silly little Canadian girl in pigtails. This is my world now. And I am an ultrarunner.

On Time and Distance

Running an ultra is like living an entire lifetime in the span of one day. You go through good times, bad times, happy times, sad times. It's truly a journey and every race changes you. It's an accomplishment that nobody can take away.

Ultrarunning introduces a kind of intensity that changes your perspective on distance, time, and emotions. You can run through rain, sun, morning, darkness, and varying kinds of terrain in a single day. You will feel as though you've lived an entire week of experiences.

Distances are different too. Suddenly you realize that cities are fairly small and it's very easy to run out of road. Plotting routes becomes increasingly difficult, and you start thinking in terms of miles or kilometers.

Once a car stopped me on one of my long runs. The driver demanded to know if I had run all the way from a certain street. I explained that I was training for a marathon. He said it was his second time seeing me, and he couldn't understand how I had come so far, so fast. Distances are shorter than we imagine.

Time carries with it a strange sensation. Five hours doesn't feel like five hours. You get home and wonder why the day is suddenly over.

Emotions fluctuate. Everything happens in extremes. You go from feeling extremely energetic and positive that you can run forever, to extremely exhausted and certain that you cannot take one more step. And yet you continue.

Near the beginning your legs are begging for rest, but after a certain distance they just move mechanically. One in front of the other, and you find that it is far less painful to run than to walk.

You learn that there are different stages of "tired". First comes a regular tired, when your heart rate is going up and you want to stop to catch your breath and rest. If you push through that, you enter a comfortable pace and a stage where it feels like you can go on forever.

Then your muscles become tired. They complain about every incline. After that your mind starts to go. You can't remember why you decided to run this far. You wonder why you chose this specific course. You tell yourself that you might not be able to make it. That you'll fail.

If you push through that, it gets better. Your muscles don't feel as tired anymore. They're a little tight, but there's no pain. Your mind starts to clear and you are only concentrating on one thing: BREATHE. So you just breathe. And push on.

All of these experiences are addictive. I have learned to favor a slower pace, but always steady and constant. When I'm running I want people to know, based on my pace, that I have been running for a very long time. And that I still have many more miles to go.

On Steve Jobs

A few days before my 29th birthday I completed my first ultra marathon distance: running 50K at a race called Mind the Ducks in New York. I ran a marathon in Toronto the next day, and qualified for The Marathon Maniacs. These were enormous accomplishments for me, and I found myself falling into a reflective and thoughtful state after it was all over. What was next for me? Where was my running going, and what were my goals in life?

The fact that I had completed a physical feat I didn't think I was capable of inspired me to re-assess my entire life and perceived potential. It called everything into question. I asked myself, "If I'm better than I imagine at running, could I also be better at life? At writing? At relationships? Have I set my sights too low?"

On my 29th birthday I watched a video of the speech Apple co-founder Steve Jobs gave at Stanford University in 2005. Jobs eloquently expressed all of my randomly floating thoughts.

He talked about connecting the dots in your life. "Trust that the dots will somehow connect in the future," he urged. As I looked back on my first 29 years, I could see a series of random and meaningless dots that were now starting to make sense.

I always wondered why my life seemed to be harder than everyone else's. Everything felt like a struggle and I was prone to feeling sorry for myself for being dealt such a poor hand. I now know that every obstacle I've encountered has made me who I am today. And I've learned to be grateful for it.

My 29th birthday was the first year that I didn't ask for a single present. Instead, I made a promise to myself: To never again feel victimized by my past. My experiences weren't handicaps. They were trials. And I connected my dots. Here they are:

1. Lonely.

I often complained of having an overprotective dad. "I wasn't allowed to do anything!" I whined. No friends. No dances. No after school activities. I spent most of my childhood alone, and for a long time I was bitter that my dad had stunted my social growth.

But his upbringing taught me to be alone. To find contentment and happiness in complete solitude. I had time to read and write and learn. Or I would go outside and explore. My imagination took on a life of its own, and there's no point experiencing life without a great imagination. Above all, I am comfortable in my own skin and in my own company.

Today, although I have friends, I don't need to be surrounded by people to be happy. Some of my greatest thoughts are still birthed in solitude. And I crave those long, lonely runs through the forest. Mentally, it has made me a stronger runner. I can be alone yet never feel sad. And I can embrace solitude with a unique affection.

2. Hungry.

The years I was hungry were dark times, but they shaped my love and appreciation for food. I remember opening unmarked metal food cans and eating whatever was in it raw—sometimes tomato sauce and sometimes plain, salty broth. Years later, I became a nutritionist.

Now every time I eat, or cook, or shop, I do so with tremendous gratitude. When I worked with clients as a nutritionist, my perspective was unique. Then later as a nutrition editor, I carried with me that point of view. I know the value of food because I know what it means to be without.

3. Stressed.

After my ex-boyfriend's brain injury, I had nothing to spare, financially or emotionally. In a state of fight or flight, I chose flight. Stress taught me to run. And it taught me to love running. To crave it. And to let it renew me.

It wasn't until running my first ultra that I started connecting these dots. And I came to a realization that reset my entire life path—that there is nothing I cannot do. I truly believed that. I learned that despite my past, I am not disadvantaged. I am not poor. I am not handicapped.

I came up with new goals for myself. Lofty ones. I knew that people weren't going to believe I could accomplish them, but people only believe what they see. I wanted to prove myself, to show what I was capable of, and to inspire that belief in others.

Steve Jobs finished his speech with the following advice: "Stay hungry. Stay foolish." I am both. So I'm on the right track.

On Specialization

In the woods, there were three animals friends who were starting school. Little Rabbit, little Bird, and little Fish. They were the best of friends, but on their first school day, their weaknesses were exposed. Rabbit was a horrible swimmer. Bird was a terrible runner. And Fish could not fly very well at all. So they were put in classes to work on their weaknesses, and they tried very hard to improve.

They practiced until Rabbit's lungs broke down in the water. Bird's little feet were exhausted on the trails. And Fish's glorious fins were destroyed when he used them as wings. Still, they practiced until they were mediocre at everything, but not particularly good at any one thing. They were also miserable.

When I refused to take Math in my senior year of high school, it was because I wasn't good at it. Instead, I took extra English credits. I was good at English. But everyone said I was making a mistake. What if I needed Math to get into college or university? What if I needed it for my first job? My rebuttal was, why the hell would I want a job where I have to do math?

I went into journalism school, where I was accepted without the math credit. Then I worked as a writer and editor. The more experience I gained, the more I specialized. I'm not qualified to do a wide range of jobs, but I'm well qualified to do the jobs I love.

The fitness and running world encourage us to improve our weaknesses. There is some wisdom to this, but we should be putting the same amount of effort, or more, into developing our strengths.

I learned early on in my running career that I was not fast. But I seemed to have a good endurance base. So instead of developing speed, I ran longer. This led me to the trails, and I discovered a new strength: I don't get hurt easily. So I boosted my mileage and got into ultrarunning.

After a few months of avoiding hard climbs or technical trails because I wasn't advanced enough as a trail runner, I took the plunge and was surprised to find that I'm actually better at the steep climbs than flatter trails. I can maintain my slow, steady pace for a long time while climbing, and that puts me on a level playing field with better athletes than me, runners who would smoke me on a flat section.

The mountains slow others down while they give me "speed." The truth is that no matter where I'm running, I go at about the same pace. So the more brutal the terrain and the steeper the grade, the more advantage I have. I started spending all my time on only focused, sustained climbing and descents. And my running dramatically improved.

On the outside, I may sometimes appear to be good at everything. But my secret is: I only do the things I'm good at. The truth is, I'm really only good at two things: writing and running. (And the running is arguable.)

But it is these two things that have weaved their way through my life, touching every aspect of it. My relationships, my physical appearance, my career, and even the country I live in.

I laugh when I see articles stating that distance running may not be ideal for weight loss. Who is doing this to lose weight? I do it because the trails feed my spirit and enhance my quality of life. They also teach me to do what I love and what I'm good at. The rest will follow.

If you were meant to fly, then fly. But if you were meant to run... go run.

On DFLs

When you want to feel inspired, who do you observe? Maybe you turn to elite athletes. Runners who race and train for first place. You might scroll to the top of your race results and admire the names you see there.

But perhaps you should do the opposite. Perhaps you should scroll down to the bottom. Here are the people who were on the course twice or three times as long as the elites. These are the people who struggled.

At some point, these runners knew they were in last place. They knew there would be no glory for them. No prizes. No fanfare. They knew that when they got to the finish line, the crowds would be gone. And yet they pushed on.

Some runners drop out when they know they will not be reaching their time goals. But not these guys. For them, the race was against themselves. They faced their demons head-on and reached out from very dark places. They didn't know how to give up.

These are my heroes.

DFL is an acronym for Dead F'ing Last. Trail runners wear that term proudly, like a badge of honor. Not because they finished last. But because they finished.

I have deep respect for DFL'ers. They were brave enough to start and stubborn enough to finish. I have had the honor of being part of a four-way DFL at the Rodeo Valley 50K, which I ran with a few friends. Two of them were in costume (Wine Girl and Beer Guy), and we stuck together the entire time, joking and laughing.

When we ran the TransRockies 6-day stage race, awards were given to the "Final Finishers" at the end of each stage, and their stories were told. I loved this. Sometimes we forget to appreciate the runners who endure the longest.

On Timed Races

I have a soft spot for timed races. Usually when I tell someone I'm doing a timed race, they react with horror and surprise. I understand that running a one-mile loop for six, 12, 24, 48, or 72 hours hardly sounds appealing. It's not easy by any means, but I find a strange comfort in it.

At a timed race, I don't have to think. I can zone out, clear my mind, and just run. I experience running in a very raw state. I'm not worried about falling, hydration, or supplies. I'm only focused on the path ahead. One foot in front of the other. Forever.

I also love them because they give newer, budding ultrarunners the opportunity to test their limits in a safe course with very little pressure. There is aid around every corner, allowing new runners to troubleshoot unexpected issues.

At Across the Years 24 Hours in Arizona, I managed to meet my baby sister as she was just about to complete 50K. She had never run an ultra distance before. I ran the last lap with her and remembered when I first set her up with a Learn to Run program. She couldn't even run for three minutes. Now she had covered a distance she could barely understand.

The ultra distance is an amazing thing. I told my sister: "No matter what has happened in your life before, or what will happen in your future, nobody can ever take that ultra away from you. When you're an ultrarunner, you're a runner forever."

You could go out the next day, join a gym and hire a personal trainer. And that trainer might not ever accomplish what you just did. You can flip through a magazine and pick out the most beautiful girl on those pages, and that girl's body might never be as strong as yours. Her legs will never carry her this far. After an ultra, you are beyond beautiful. You are unbreakable.

My sister would end up covering more than 40 miles that day, logging more than 100K during her entire stay with us over the holidays. She hadn't trained for this, previously running five miles a week or less. But I knew she had an ultra in her.

As I watched the other runners, I was inspired by so many fearlessly circling that one-mile loop. All different ages, different shapes, different goals. There were people who looked like they were 80 years old, and there was one 8-year-old boy who ended up with more than 30 miles. People were slow, but consistent.

One foot in front of the other. And they just never stopped.

I was amazed at the strength and resilience of the human spirit, and it seemed almost unfair to me that strong souls should reside in weak bodies. Why can't our bodies keep up with the resolve of our spirits?

Earlier on, I met Sarah. Sarah was a pretty girl with long dreads, running in minimalist Merrell shoes. We stopped to ask her how long she had been running in them. She was embarrassed to say — only 12 miles.

It turned out that it was actually her husband who had registered for this race, but he had become injured and could no longer run. She agreed to take his spot, even though she was only training for her first half marathon. She thought she'd take it easy, run a few laps, and see how she felt.

Sarah would take a break every so often to breastfeed her youngest child before jumping back on the course. She ended up with more than 50K.

This race had a mail system that allowed friends at home to send encouraging notes. In many of the motivational messages I received, people wrote that I was an inspiration. But these are the people who inspire me. I've done the training, planned the course, and eased into ultrarunning like an old man slipping into a chilly pool. But these guys came up to a mountain they had never seen, and looked up at it without the slightest fear. Then they said, "Meh... What the hell." And dove right in. Just one foot in front of the other. Forever.

On Why We Run

Why we run has been the topic of countless running articles, blog posts, and general musings. When I first started running, I found the question kind of strange. Nobody asks why people get on ellipticals. Why they swim. Why they bike to the park. Why should running be any different?

As I started getting into ultrarunning and especially when I trained for and ran my first 100-miler, the question made more sense. It was easier to see why people would wonder.

With the increase of mileage and the obsession with harsher terrain and more brutal climbs, the running difficulty shot up and the perceived rewards from a non-runner's perspective were few:

- There was no longer a significant weight loss benefit.
- The difficulty level wasn't fun or pleasant.
- The physical repercussions like lost toenails and blisters look excruciating.
- The time commitment was extreme.
- The risk of injury was high.

And yet I was still reluctant to answer the question of why. Because the truth is, I didn't really know why. And I still haven't found a logical answer.

I actually believe that there is no good reason for running 100 miles. But I also believe that I don't need one. I love the distance. I love training for and running 100s. And that is enough. I don't need to lose weight from it and I don't need to earn money from it. Yes, ultrarunning is senseless and crazy and dangerous. That's sort of the point. I just need to run.

We live in a world where everything requires a purpose and an explanation, or else it's useless. Exercise must have a direct benefit in order to be worth our time. Not surprisingly, we are more sickly and sedentary than ever.

Instead of going outside, we sit around and reason that there is not enough of a physical or financial benefit in ultrarunning. But I believe ultrarunning is more of an art than a job.

Nobody asks:

- Why we go to the theatre
- Why we listen to an orchestra
- Why we visit art galleries
- Why we appreciate music

Or for that matter:

- Why go to a movie on opening night?
- Why watch a sunrise?
- Why pet a puppy?

There is no logic or reason behind these things, yet they somehow feed our souls. They make us human.

As a friend once told me, we need people to run 100 miles just as we need people who can sing above an orchestra, or who can paint a masterpiece. It proves to us the wonder and versatility of humanity, and reminds us that as a species we are capable of extraordinary feats.

And so we need an army of runners who can move swiftly with no purpose. Who seek out trails that lead to nowhere. Who scale mountains just to see the other side. More importantly, we need things in our lives that we don't have to rationalize. Things we can just love recklessly. And we need to stop asking why.

Ultrarunning makes me human. It's the one thing I don't need to explain.

On Excuses

An ultra can do a lot of things for a lot of people. But one thing it will always do is change your mind. It will focus your perspective and help you see things as they really are. Here are some common excuses that may be clouding your vision:

1. I can't run an ultra yet — I'm not in my best shape.

I've seen some epic love handles and beer bellies cross the finish line at several ultras. And although not all runners are visibly out of shape, many do have a target area that is far from perfect — flabby bits or underdeveloped muscles. If you're waiting to be in the best shape of your life, you will never run an ultra.

Running with extra weight is far from easy, whether it is bulky muscle weight or fat. But weight has almost no effect on your potential to cross the finish line. This finish line is about mental strength and raw determination. Don't worry about achieving perfect fitness. The more you run ultras, the more your body will adapt to running ultras. Then before you know it, your body will be perfect... for running ultras.

2. My first ultra will be just like my training runs.

You haven't the slightest clue what your first ultra will be like. Expect nothing. The veteran standing beside you doesn't know what this race will be like either. Neither does the guy who has run this course ten times. He can tell you about his past experiences, but he can't tell you what the run will be like today. That's the beauty of ultrarunning: Anything can happen.

Simulate race day conditions during training, but never let it fool you into thinking that you now know exactly what's coming. The weather could turn, your food could run out, or you could step on a rattlesnake. Who knows?

Instead of stressing about it, take it as a relief. There's no pressure to be completely prepared, because nobody is. The runners who thrive are the ones who can be flexible. Have a good base, don't forget your nutrition, and know how to adapt. Be ready and willing to tweak your strategy at a moment's notice, and never see change as a failure.

3. I can't run an ultra — I don't have any support.

Support — race crew, pacers, friends dragging your stuff around — is a big deal among ultrarunners, but not having support can't be used as an excuse. Ultimately, only you are responsible for your failure or success. Yes, pacers and crews make things easier.

They are convenient and invaluable. But you don't need a small army to pull off a finish.

In fact, many newbies don't have any support at all. It's not until you start running several ultras and make friends in the ultra community that people become willing to hang out and support you.

Emotional and moral support are another issue. Never expect to go into your first ultra with the full support of all your non-running friends and family. Even your running friends may have a hard time believing in you.

Do you know when people start believing in you? When you prove yourself. When you finish. When you find success. So don't sit around whining about how nobody supports you. Why should they? You haven't done a thing. Your ultra is still just crazy talk.

Know your potential and go after it with all your strength. When you believe in yourself and prove your ability to finish, others will start believing in you as well.

4. If I'm running in the back of the pack, I'm in the wrong training group.

Take it from this back-of-the-packer—you're in the perfect spot. When I first moved to San Diego, I was always in the back of the pack. As I slowly started becoming a mid-packer, I sought out stronger runners who would push me to the back again.

Many runners are embarrassed or ashamed to bring up the rear, to the point that they will switch training groups. But I'm not here to impress anyone—

I'm here to get better, and I want to do it as quickly as possible.

Struggling to keep up with a strong group is how I've grown. I've picked up tips and invaluable knowledge that might have taken me years to learn otherwise, and it also keeps me extremely humble.

Obviously there's a limit — you don't want people waiting forever for you to catch up. But your own common sense and/or pride will prevent you from hitting any extremes. Don't be one of those runners who are only a few minutes behind the second-last person, assume the group is too fast for them, and leave.

I want people in front of me, driving me forward. I want to be friends with people who can kick my ass any day of the week, who are better trained, and have more experience. The rewards are far better in last place than in first.

5. I'm too old to start running ultras.

At 30, I'm a newborn in this sport. I'm also one of the slowest, less experienced, and least accomplished. Ultrarunning is for an older crowd. The strongest runners tend to be in their 40s and 50s (women included), with a few in their 60s who can run circles around me. I've seen past-middle-aged men with abs more ripped than any teenager.

Age in ultrarunning means grace, wisdom, and respect. You are admired and consulted for advice. If you watch an older ultrarunner, there is a calm and carefree aura around them. It's like they know every step of every trails, what's underneath every rock, and the location of every bug.

Their sense of direction is sharp, and you get the feeling that if you were to ditch them in the middle of nowhere on the other side of the world, they would run back and ring your doorbell in about a week. Other sports cut you off after a certain age. In this sport, you become a legend.

6. After I finish an ultra, everyone will admire and praise me.

Ultrarunning is like a spiritual experience — you get the most out of it when you approach it with a pure and humble heart. An ultra is something you can't finish for anyone else. You have to do it for yourself.

The runners who give off a "Hey, look at me!" vibe generally don't stick with ultras. If your goal is social acceptance and praise, there are much easier ways to get it.

When you run a marathon, all your non-running family and friends think you're a superstar. They might meet you at the finish line, talk about you with pride, and tell you how awesome you are.

But when you run an ultra, you are out on those trails by yourself. You're facing your challenges alone on a terrain that is foreign. There are no motivational signs to lift your spirits. There are no cheering fans to scream your name. If you're lucky, you might get some weak claps or cheers at the finish line.

But that finish is unlike anything else. It's yours and yours alone. Nobody can know what it took for you to get there, and nobody can share in your full victory. That finish line is where you first realize that you can do anything.

You'll go into the world the next day to brag about your accomplishments, but instead of looking at you with admiration, people will look at you like you're insane. Your non-running friends will not understand. Their first reaction will probably not be, "You're awesome!"

If it's a nod from society you're looking for, run a marathon. But if it's a life-changing experience of personal strength and perseverance that you want, finish an ultra.

7. It doesn't appear that anyone else is struggling as much as I am. I must not belong.

I saw a video recently that completely changed my perspective on running. I can't remember where I saw it. It was one of those things you watch casually, and don't realize until weeks later that it was a turning point for you.

This video was an interview with a seasoned, elite ultrarunner talking about a race. The distance was significant; I think it was 100 miles. He talked about finishing the first 26 miles, and feeling wiped. He casually mentioned being tired as if it was a normal thing, but I thought, "Wait a minute. He's an ultra-elite. He gets tired after a marathon??"

When I get tired at 26 miles, I used to attribute it to the fact that I wasn't conditioned. I was a newbie and probably out of shape. I was in over my head. But here was a veteran with years of solid races under his belt, still feeling tired at 26 miles. It forced me to change my perspective.

Around the same time, I read the book *AWOL on the Appalachian Trail* where David Miller recounts his experience hiking the entire Appalachian. He recalls a day when he was struggling up a hill, passed some other hikers, and was shocked to hear them admire his speed and agility. He felt terrible.

He writes:

Everyone sweats; everyone pants for breath. The person who is in better shape will usually push himself to hike more quickly and bump into the same limitations. But when a fit person is stressed, he is less likely to attribute the difficulty to his shortcomings... Obviously conditioning is advantageous, but the perception of disadvantage can be more debilitating than the actual disadvantage.

Ultras are hard for everyone. Ultras are just plain hard. Everyone struggles up that hill. Everyone has trouble breathing. Everyone feels the hot sun. Everyone is sweating. Everyone wants to sit down.

You — reading this book — would not be any worse off than I am on a steep, rocky hill. Trails can't tell whether you're an elite or a newbie. They'll challenge you just the same. So you belong here just as much as I do. And I belong here just as much as the person who wins first place.

The ultra distance is hard to get your mind around. That's why people give ultrarunners puzzled looks. But once you break down that wall, run your first ultra, run your second ultra, and then realize you're hooked — all those lies you believed about yourself are exposed. And it's easier to see yourself as you really are—strong, courageous, and able.

On Introversion

My pre-school teacher tried to have me put into a special needs class. She was my first real contact with the outside world, and convinced there was something wrong with me. I was uncharacteristically quiet, and showed very little interest in participating with the rest of the class. I mostly just sat in the corner and stared. But my mom insisted there was nothing wrong with me and refused the transfer. My mom said that I was just introverted and that was okay.

Western society views introversion as a negative quality, but I couldn't disagree more. I love being introverted. I have a unique way of looking at the world, though I understand my limitations. While I can make an effort to get out of my comfort zone, true success lies in focusing on my strongest qualities.

I'm very analytical and I thrive in solitude. Being alone helps me develop new ideas and leave a mark on this world through writing, far more than socializing in a group. In person, I am soft spoken, laid back, and silly with my closest friends. I am highly inquisitive, creative, and sensitive to my environment.

I spent a lot of time alone as a child. I was intrigued by my surroundings and fascinated by new objects or situations. Details mesmerized me and I enjoyed sitting in a corner for hours, just watching and observing. Not many understood this about me.

While my pre-school teacher was convinced I had a learning disability, at home I was already reading and writing. Since I had no children's books, I would immerse myself in my mom's ESL books and my dad's seminary textbooks.

At the library, I would plant myself in one spot and read every single book on the shelf, one after the other in the order they were shelved. When it was time to leave, I would come back another day and pick up exactly where I had left off. I wanted to read every book in the library. It didn't matter what they were about. It only mattered that I was reading.

Outdoors, I found peaceful solitude. I would play outside for hours and pretend it was a forest. My imagination ran wild.

Years later when I started running trails, I was overwhelmed with all the sights and sounds and textures. I drank everything in with joy in my heart, and ran the same route over and over, learning new details about it on every run. I would stop to flip and peek underneath rocks, or climb trees. I would bend over and scoop up dirt to feel its texture. No detail was too trivial or insignificant.

I have wondered in the past whether I might be mildly autistic in some way, because I am sensitive to overstimulation. I don't like loud noises. I hate crowds. I don't like malls. I enjoy having one task and pouring myself into it completely until it is finished.

I can come up with some unique perspectives, but I stress with common, daily activities that are second nature to most people—like driving a car. My thoughts are like spaghetti and every strand intertwines with thousands of others. I compare and contrast things that have nothing apparent in common. I find connections and I write them down. Doing this is important to me.

As a teenager, I would fantasize about being invisible. I wanted to observe and be present in social situations, but didn't want to make small talk. My ex used to accuse me of being anti-social, but nothing could be further from the truth. I just like to take my time. If you put one person in front of me, I am very dedicated to getting to know them and open up easily. It's easy for me to talk to someone as if we're the only ones on the planet because in my focused mindspace, we are.

I'm terrible at parties. It's information overload, and I feel anxious. If I could sit in a corner at a party and talk to only one new person, I would be in heaven. But I don't know how to work a room. I don't know how or when to move on to the next person when there are still so many things I don't know about the person I'm currently talking to.

Trail running sifts people out for me, and I am infinitely grateful for that. Running single track, I am never mobbed by people. For me, being in the wilderness is like getting a massage or hearing my favorite song. My mind and my body immediately relax. My muscles loosen up. And I can breathe again.

Large-scale marathons, on the other hand, are a nightmare for me. It is clear to me that I don't belong on streets, in a big city, or in any crowded place.

My happiest moments have been when I've felt as though I were alone on the planet: moments of solitude in the Grand Canyon, or sprinting through the woods alongside a red fox. Although I do enjoy the company of others, I need a lot of alone time to feel balanced and fulfilled.

My boyfriend Shacky is low-key, a quality I need in a partner. We both like food and trail running and can easily do all the fun stuff together and not worry about dinner parties or large gatherings.

When we do have a larger gathering, it's actually fun with Shacky. In a crowded place, he has a calming effect on me, and I feel like we can go anywhere. He's also slightly more social than me, and he brings me out of my shell in a positive way. This helps me keep a good balance in my life, as opposed to doing something nuts like moving into a cave.

When I ran my first 100-miler, I thought I could do it without pacers. I hadn't had much practice with talking during running, and I worried that having someone there would contribute to overstimulation, giving me something else to worry about. I have never had any issues with motivation, so I didn't feel I needed a pacer in that regard. I knew that I was driven to finish the race, and I trusted that I had what it takes to get there.

But at mile 80 something flipped in my brain, and I realized I wanted to finish with Shacky. I became obsessed with catching him and finishing together. I didn't want to finish alone. It was suddenly extremely important that I not finish alone.

I put my head down and ran eight-minute miles in the last 20 miles of the race, to catch up to Shacky who was far ahead of me. I caught him coming toward me on the out-and-back, and he agreed to walk while I finished my loop and caught up.

I crossed the line with Shacky by my side, feeling a desperation for human company that I had never felt before. That day I learned that stripped down to my most raw form, even though I am an introvert, I can still use a good running buddy.

On Running 100 Miles

My love for distance was something I fed privately at first. Unlogged, unaccompanied long runs in the woods. I'd disappear while it was still dark and everyone was asleep, sneaking back just as they were waking up. Nobody really knew how long I was out there. I'd run marathon distances on my own, or I'd disappear down by the lake for hours.

But 100 miles seemed like a fantasy, something like the way people dream of winning the lottery. I wondered what kind of person I would have to be to complete 100 miles. What kind of mental focus I'd need, and what kind of runners I would have to surround myself with.

The 100 is a distance that intrigued me for years. I always imagined that when I finished 100 miles, I'd be at the peak of my physical conditioning, near-elite status. What other challenge could be harder?

Now I know better.

I know that 100 miles is not a distance that belongs to the elite. I have seen people finish 100s who are overweight. Senior citizens. People who have barely trained. People who have never run a marathon. People who registered by mistake. Sometimes people who don't even really like running.

The ultra is an equalizer. It strips away the mystery surrounding the athletes we admire, and it puts us on their level. It lets us shake their hands and pace alongside them.

Where marathons force you into corrals based on your speed, the ultra slaps you on the back and says, "Stand wherever the hell you want. Your chance is as good as any of these other poor suckers." And when you believe that, you know you're an ultrarunner.

We idolize speed more than we should, and we forget about endurance. We admire the stereotypical "runner's body" and we know in our hearts that we will never look like that. So we resign ourselves to shorter distances, shorter training runs, and a defeated approach to running. That is a mistake.

One hundred miles is just ground and earth and mud and space. It is all the things we already know, and it belongs to all of us. We can walk it, we can run it, and with enough time we can cover it. It's public domain.

My first 100 was like a coming out. It was a validation. A declaration that this is who I am and this is what I can do. And I'm going to keep doing it.

On Running the Grand Canyon

I leap off the rock where I am sitting and grab a large stone. Clutching it as a weapon, I scream at Shacky to come back, or for god's sake to pick up a weapon.

This is not our first encounter with wildlife. But it is the first time I feel compelled to pick up a weapon. It's almost one-thirty in the morning and we're close to the top of the South Rim of the Grand Canyon.

Less than a mile ago, I was slogging behind Shacky when I heard him hooting, hollering and clapping. At first, I thought he had reached the top. But as I turned the switchback, my blood turned cold when he told me to stand back—there was a mountain lion on the rock ahead, glaring and crouching toward us.

The switchback was set up in such a way that we would have to give our backs to the hungry cat in order to continue on the trail—something you never, ever do. So we tried our best to walk backwards up the trail, making loud noises to keep the animal away. Even after we had walked some distance, I was watching my back, certain I was only seconds from death.

A few minutes later, I had stopped dead in my tracks to see a huge deer staring into my face on my left hand side. It was so close I could touch it. It was a beautiful creature, and I yelled at Shacky to give me the camera. But Shacky didn't think it was a good idea—the deer didn't look too pleased and he said that they attack if they feel threatened. I backed away as quickly and quietly as I could.

As I turned away, I heard rocks fall behind me. I spun around and saw the deer had followed me, blocking the trail behind me and staring me down. Oh crap. We kept walking straight.

The next second, we almost stumbled into another deer blocking the trail in front of us. A deer in front. A deer behind. Both unafraid. There was nowhere to go.

I suggested we sit down and wait, to see if they would move. We sat. We waited. After what seemed like 10 minutes, it was clear the deer were not moving. I suggested we toss some pebbles at their feet, to make noise and hopefully scare them away.

That was when Shacky started throwing rocks right at it. I yelled at him to stop and hid my face, certain the deer would attack. Dear God. This is how I will die, I think. Death by deer. Only steps away from finishing our run.

Shacky finally got mad at waiting so long, and lunged toward the deer to push it off the trail. That's when I grabbed the rock thinking, I will now have to bludgeon Bambi to death with my bare hands.

As Shacky approached, the deer just grunted and bounded away. My adrenaline was so high, I just want to get the hell out of the canyon.

The entire final climb for us has been in the dark. We can no longer see the inspiration of the canyon, and although the moon is brilliant, the rocks often obscure it as we trudge through switchback after never-ending switchback.

We had started the morning in much better spirits. The original plan was for our group to start at 3:30 a.m.

to avoid the heat of the day, but Gordy thought that was a mistake.

Gordon Ainsleigh, the godfather of ultrarunning, had come along with us to run his first-ever R2R2R, a non-stop double crossing of the Grand Canyon. Gordy was the first man who believed it was possible to run 100 miles in one day, and proved it.

Many on the trail recognized him from the movie *Unbreakable*, or as the first man to run Western States 100. But really — he invented Western States 100.

We can see nothing ahead or behind us, so it is impossible to tell how much trail we have left. I think of Gordon Ainsleigh's story about Ron Kelley, who attempted to run 100 miles of the Western States course right after Gordy did, and gave up after 97 miles. "He didn't know how close he was," Gordy said. And that's how I feel now.

I know the end is close, but I don't know when it will come.

What intrigues me about Gordy is his limitless spirit. He doesn't see boundaries when it comes to running. Not for distance, not for speed, and not for temperature. Gordy shrugged off the heat of the Canyon, and said he wanted to start at dawn.

The 3:30 a.m. group would be going down South Kaibab in the dark, missing some of the most breathtaking views of the Canyon. The climb up Bright Angel, Gordy argued, wasn't as scenic and we wouldn't miss much doing that in the dark instead. Gordy was here to experience the Canyon and he thought an early start would be a mistake.

He talked us into joining him. Shacky was reluctant, because both heat and elevation are issues he struggles with. But I was eager to follow Gordy. This was a once-in-a-lifetime opportunity, running into the Canyon with a legend, and I wasn't about to let it slip away.

Gordy also convinced our friend Christine to come along, so on Saturday morning Gordy, Shacky, Christine and I all hopped in the van. Then we sat there as we realized that none of us knew how to get to the trailhead.

Gordy was not the least bit concerned. In fact, he didn't worry about much of anything on the entire trip. He munched on an orange and told us to just drive. Eventually we did find the trailhead, though I'm still not sure how we got there.

When we arrived at the parking lot, we didn't see the van of the 3:30 a.m. group, so that worried us a little. Gordy just shrugged and said, "Don't worry about that." As it turned out, the early group got dropped off and the van was driven back.

Gordy wasn't worried about water either. None of us knew were all the water stops were, and we carried a ton of water. Gordy had just two handhelds and didn't seem the least bit concerned. After Phantom Ranch, he would even convince Christine to dump some of her own water to lighten her load and run faster. She was reluctant.

"But I need water!"

"You can get water any time you want!" said Gordy.

"No! I cannot get water any time I want!"

"You can always just drink from the river. If you get sick, it won't be until next week or the week after."

All that matters to Gordy is today. This run. Right now.

Christine was not one to drink from the river, but she did dump some water, and it did help her run faster. In fact, she finished the run ahead of us all and even ended up sharing her water with Gordy when he took a fall and spilled his own supply.

Christine and Gordy did stick together for the most part, and Christine rolled her eyes every time someone would delay them to take a picture of Gordy or try to chat with him.

"Don't you want my picture??" she joked. "I am famous where I am from!" So they would take her picture too.

"Come on Gordy, time to go!" she would say when he stopped to sit or talk for too long.

I took an early lead coming down South Kaibab. The stunning views made me catch my breath and thank God that we had had the sense to start in the daylight. To say it was beautiful is an understatement. The Grand Canyon is not a place. It is an experience. It cannot be described. It must be lived.

The rock carvings descending for miles, with splashes of red and orange and brown against the sunrise are enough to make you believe in God. Animals unafraid of human contact, fiery red sand slowly camouflaging your shoes and gear, cold caves and crevices offering the odd relief from the hot sun — it's a different world. It's a wonderland.

Every picture I took, I knew would not do the scenery justice. I couldn't fit the entire landscape in my camera. I could focus on the runner, but not on the towering boulders above his head. I could focus on the rock, but not on the ant-sized conga line of runners traversing it.

But the most striking quality of the Canyon is its ability to put your life into perspective. In the Canyon, you are tiny and insignificant. A mere speck in the enormous and overwhelming beauty of this place. None of your issues matter here. None of your problems make sense. All that matters are these rocks. And all you see is the Canyon.

Maybe once or twice in your life, you experience a run this joyous. I couldn't help but running down that canyon as fast as I could, stopping dead every so often to let the others catch up. Gordy would later tell me I had "the happiest stride in ultrarunning."

I felt like a bird that had just been set free. At one point, making the descent from the North Rim, I was so far ahead of the others, it felt like I was all alone on the planet, just doing a training run at one of the seven wonders of the world.

It is runs like these — not money, and not assets — that make me filthy rich. I felt like I owned everything around me. I was swimming in riches. Running fast was an expression of gratitude and joy. Like a child dashing toward her favorite swing, this was my playground.

Of course, the uphills weren't as fast. I hiked many of the inclines, focusing on keeping a steady stride and a respectable cadence. If I looked up suddenly, the canyons would make me dizzy. So I looked down and tried to stay ahead of Shacky.

Shacky wasn't having a good day. He wanted to turn back before reaching the North Rim, but I refused to let him. I wondered later if I should have let him, since he was sick on the way back. He was having trouble with the heat and elevation, and had a rough time keeping any food down. A few times, he had to lie on his back to keep from puking, or put his head down in the shade.

I stayed with him until I was certain he would not turn back, and then let him make the last part of the final climb up to the North Rim on his own. At the top, he was miserable and out of water.

The water source at the top of the North Rim was shut off, and it was a mile round trip to the ranger station for a refill. Just as I was preparing to make the water run, a car pulled into the parking lot.

"Are you guys running R2R2R?" someone called out.

We looked up to see a young couple who decided to make a little trail magic happen by driving up with some water. They had enough for both Shacky and me. I thanked them profusely. We chatted for a few minutes—they were aspiring ultrarunners, and they wanted their picture taken with Gordy as well. (Christine made sure they took one of her too.)

When we finally took off, I felt amazing. Shacky was feeling better and I hoped the worst was over. We agreed to meet at Phantom Ranch, just before the final climb, and I took off ahead. I was running at a good pace, and passed a handful of groups—two sets of runners and three groups of hikers. The stretch was long and desert-like, but I do well in the heat and I was still mesmerized by the glory of the Canyon.

I pulled into Phantom Ranch not long after Gordy and Christine. They were filling up their supplies and getting ready to leave. Shacky arrived just a few minutes later, but he wasn't looking good.

He lay down in the dirt and I noticed he was shaking. His legs were shaking, and so was his head. I freaked out and brought up the possibility of spending the night at Phantom Ranch. He refused.

So we sat at Phantom Ranch until he was able to eat enough calories to make the climb. It took him a while to keep anything down. We were there for almost an hour. All the hiking groups and the runners I had passed came through and left before us.

One group of hikers was finishing the R2R2R— they had started at 2 a.m. that morning. They wanted to set the record for youngest and oldest to complete the R2R2R in one party—the boy was 17 and the oldest gentleman was 67.

"I dunno, I'm worried about that Western States guy," the 17-year-old said. "He looks like he's 95."

"Gordy's 64," I replied.

"Oh good."

Before they left, he waved goodbye and said, "I'm pretty sure I'll die out there." They made it to the top before us.

I was really worried about Shacky, but as soon as the sun went down, he was ready to go. In fact, he was like a new runner.

Shacky is a moonchild. He comes alive at night. I'm the opposite—I die with the setting of the sun. I pulled out my headlamp and prepared for what I expected would be a long hike to the top.

One of the campers called out behind us, "We'll pray for you!". I guess we looked pretty beat up.

But Shacky was picking up the pace, rejuvenated by nightfall. I tried to run, but realized I was exhausted. Too much fast running followed by long waits. I was burned out.

There are two ways you can come up the South rim: via the Kaibab trail where we had descended, or via Bright Angel trail.

Bright Angel is longer, but less steep, and that's what we opted for. In my mind, "longer but less steep" meant that it would be a steady incline. I was okay with that. Instead, I found the trail relatively flat to begin, even making slight descents for the first few miles. This irritated me because it was time on my feet without really getting me to my destination.

My fatigue translated into frustration with the trail and with my headlamp. Every time I looked, up, the top of the canyon looked no closer. Why weren't we climbing? I wanted to get to the top and be finished.

When the climbing finally began, my headlamp was playing games with me. I couldn't gauge the depth of the path, so I'd find myself either stumbling, or expecting a big step where it was flat. I came down hard on my ankles a few times, misjudging my landings, and I was getting irritated.

Halfway up, I remembered I had a hand-held light, and used that instead. I could finally see the shadows on the trail, and moving forward was much easier on my body. I kept my head down since I'd start to feel dizzy every time I looked up. I was worried about tipping right off the Canyon.

In the distance, we could see groups of tiny headlamps inching their way to the top. It was impossible to judge how far we had left to go, and neither of us had a watch. When night came to the Canyon, all inspiration left me. I could no longer admire the rock walls. I could no longer see the rich ground at my feet. I wanted the sun to come back, or I wanted to be done.

I was holding Shacky back. He was full of energy and had to keep waiting for me to catch up. We both had trouble eating now, but Shacky faithfully stopped to get his calories in, while I blew them off.

The more time passed, the more miserable I felt. It was this final climb that made this one of the toughest runs I have ever done. A familiar feeling of exhaustion swept over me—it felt like the last three miles of my first 100. Pure torture.

This was slightly worse because there were scorpions at our feet and bats flying over our heads, making me jumpy. My nerves were shot.

That was when I heard Shacky ahead of me clapping and yelling again. "Come here! Hurry up!" Oh no, I thought, there's another mountain lion. He's calling me so we can die together. But it turned out to be the top. We made it! We're done!

It wasn't until the next day when I started to appreciate the full extent of our victory, and what an amazing thing we had done. For weeks later, when I closed my eyes to sleep at night, all I could see was the Canyon.

Those red walls towering over me, carved to perfection with the sun travelling across the sky. In my dreams, I am still running down that dirt road. Still splashing the Colorado River water on my face. A part of me will always long for the Canyon. Until I can see it again.

On Caballo Blanco

If you've read *Born to Run*, you're familiar with the late Caballo Blanco, or Micah True. Caballo was one of my early running inspirations. He had a spirit that could not be matched.

A nomadic and elusive trail runner, Caballo embraced running in its purest sense. He ran for the sheer joy of it. Not to compete in races. Not to log his runs. Not to improve his training. He ran because he loved it. Period.

As our race schedules fill up and we pursue PRs, will we still remember the joy of bounding over a mountain for no reason at all? Will we forget how to run as Caballo did, or will his death inspire us to honor his spirit?

I am saddened when I see articles and books with headlines like, *Run Less, Run Faster!* If you want to run less, you should just run less. Running is not supposed to a chore. It likely isn't your full-time job. If it doesn't bring you joy and renewal, why waste your time?

In Caballo's honor, I encourage you to run once this week without logging it as a workout, or thinking of it as training. Don't track your mileage and don't time yourself. Pay attention to your surroundings, have compassion for the life around you, and work to protect and preserve your trails as well as the people who run them.

The spirit of ultrarunning must always embrace selflessness, generosity, adventure, and strength. These are things that cannot die. When I am running in the mountains, I think of Caballo. And when I am racing, I recite this poem my friend Trisha wrote about Caballo after his death:

Run close to the mountains
Stay a heartbeat away
Cover the low moon with your wings
And walk tomorrow's miles today

Watch the sun race the sky
And know you'll pass her once again

When time frees your soul and you find
The fabled trail that doesn't end

Dust ascends on the horizon
A deep, rumbling thunder without rain
The sound of rampant hearts, a legion
Earthly, feral and unconstrained

The search will end as it began
A trail of footprints, a bird and a feather
When a white horse dies on a sandy road
All wild hearts mourn together

On Suffering

I registered for my second 100-mile race, Javelina 100, on a whim. I was already registered for Chimera 100 three weeks after Javelina, so I thought it would be too risky to run two 100-mile races that close together. But come race day, a few of my runner friends encouraged me to register, and I decided to go for it.

I ended up finishing close to two hours faster than my first 100, and I felt 100 percent better. I was fully recovered two days later, and in high spirits. It gave me the confidence I needed going into Chimera, and a boost of positive energy.

But going into Javelina, I anticipated suffering. In the early miles, I thought about suffering in-depth, and tried to mentally prepare myself for what would come. The truth is, there is always some degree of suffering when you're running 100 miles.

It would seem that one of the main goals in our society is to avoid suffering, and yet suffering is part of what we crave as ultrarunners. It's a big part of what makes our victory so sweet.

When I feel better at the end of an ultra than I did at my last race, I don't think it's because I've become significantly faster or stronger. The main difference is that I'm more familiar with the discomfort. Instead of bothering me, it has become something I enjoy and even crave. I seek that suffering.

Growing up in the church, one common question that was asked of us was, "If God is love, why does he allow suffering?" But is suffering in itself really the problem? It is because of suffering that people do amazing things. I imagine a life of complete comfort would make us sick, bored, and miserable.

And yet there are so many who are suffering needlessly. People who suffer against their will, at the hands of others. Or those who suffer as a result of their environment, at the hands of an illness, or because of the way they were born.

Then there are those who suffer for causes they believe in. There are martyrs, or those who take a stand. So many before me suffered far worse than I do, to fight for something worthy.

I decided that I would be grateful for my 100-mile suffering. I am lucky because this is a suffering that I choose. It is not suffering I cannot control. It is something I picked and even paid for. It was my choice, and for that reason far easier to bear.

I need obstacles in life. Something to strive for. I'm not a stranger to suffering in life, but this is the first time I have been in completely control of how much I suffer. I can pull the plug at any time, or I can challenge myself physically and push my body to new levels. That is so rare. I choose my poison and can drink it gladly.

My mantra for the rest of the race became, "I chose this." It reminded me to bear my suffering with joy. And for the entire race, joy was what I found.

On Making a Difference

Slab City was first described to me as place where people go to hide from the government. Previously a military base in California, this plot of land was abandoned and is now home to several homeless, meth addicts, and people who for whatever reason wish to live off the grid. Occasional fights over public space break out. There are no rules here. There is also no electricity, no running water, no sewers, no toilets, and no trash pickup service.

As you enter, you are greeted by a homemade sign: THE LAST FREE PLACE, and later another one — WELCOME TO SLAB CITY. Here you will find donkeys, dogs, naked hippies with painted faces, drug dealers, and make-shift homes in the middle of nowhere.

An abandoned ambulance has been turned into a residence. So has a school bus. A barefoot dude wanders around with a beer in one hand while a girl with hairy legs and exposed tits says hello. And then you see a brilliant bomb of paint—a mountain of spectacular colors. That is Salvation Mountain.

Elaborate nooks, crannies, and tree branches stretch like wild things all through the mountain, covered in rainbows of inspirational and biblical messages. The mountain is three stories high and as wide as a football field. You can climb right to the top.

Corners that at first appear empty open up to elaborate memorials, intricately decorated to honor various dead with messages of love and longing. Unlike most works of art, here you are welcome to enter, climb, touch, and participate.

The entire mountain is Leonard Knight's work of art. A simple man who may never have caused a ripple in civilized society, but is famous here. Adored, revered, and respected. A small voice in the desert. The message he most prominently displays: God Is Love.

Leonard says, "I painted the mountain because I love God and I love people." And the people come to see it.

I smile to think of so many of us stuck in our churches talking about a way to "change the world," yet blending into our comfortable surroundings. We believe we need to be rich or famous or deeply talented to make a real difference or stand out. But in the dark places—in the shunned corners like Slab City, even the smallest flicker burns with the power of a blowtorch.

To me, Salvation Mountain is proof that anyone can make a difference. Not with eloquence or intelligence. But with child-like stripes, circles, and three simple words: God Is Love.

On Ultrarunner Narcissism

One of the topics of discussion I've had with other ultrarunners is whether or not we should be considered selfish for our dedication to this sport. Ultrarunning takes up a lot of time, both in training and in racing. It takes a toll on our bodies, our families, and saps our energy. Is it worth putting ourselves through this for "no good reason"? Are we really all just a bunch of narcissists?

Here are my four thoughts on the subject:

1. You can tell who the narcissists are.

People come in all shapes, sizes, and intentions. Yes, there are people who run with a narcissistic vibe. But there are others who do it humbly, graciously, and with a giving spirit. It's easy to pick out the narcissists:

- A narcissist will tout his own accomplishments. A humble runner will call out the accomplishments of others.
- A narcissist is all about bragging on social media, and will hijack the posts of others to report their own (irrelevant) mileage. A humble runner will use social media to inspire and encourage others toward their goals.
- A narcissist will speed by his competitors whenever possible. A humble runner will encourage the

people he passes, and motivate them to follow.

- A narcissist will be eager to offer you advice you didn't ask for, and assume you are much less accomplished than she is. A humble runner will relate to you on your level.

- A narcissist will make excuses for their failures. He will blame the course, the volunteers, the Race Director, or just say he wasn't trying very hard. A humble runner learns from his mistakes.

- A narcissist says "Look what I did!" A humble runner says, "If I can do it, so can you."

A few examples:

a) At Ridgecrest 50K, my friend Shawna was having a low point when Raul passed her. Raul kept waving her along, gesturing her to follow him, and that's how they got to the finish line together. Shawna PR'd her 50K that day.

b) Ed Ettinghausen runs countless 100s and is always on hand to wait for and cheer the last runner on the course. Those who have run 100s know how gross and tired you feel after you cross the finish line. All you want to do is change your clothes, take a shower, and pass out. You're cold and miserable. Everything hurts. Now imagine sitting around for hours after that, in your own filth and fatigue, waiting for the very last runner to come in. Imagine cheering for them loudly and genuinely, a person you don't even know. That's Ed.

c) At the inaugural Mogollon Monster 100, the winner of the race, Jamil Coury, was trotting along when he came across an elderly couple on the side of the road with a flat tire. He stopped running to make sure they were safe, and ended up taking several minutes to change their tire in the middle of the course. The couple was later shocked to learn that he was racing, since he took his time to make sure they were cared for and never complained about the delay.

d) Jesse Haynes was in first place (and went on to win) the San Juan 50K when he passed Shelly and me. We were lost and obviously in the wrong place ahead of him. He stopped dead in his tracks to help us and offer directions, not hesitating to break his stride for a couple of clueless runners.

e) Again at Ridgecrest 50K, I was crashing in the final miles. I was walking and feeling sorry for myself when Catra Corbett powered past me and yelled, "Let's go, girl! We got this!" I ran after her. I crossed the finish line right behind her with a new PR, a sub-6 finish. And I got an award for first in my age group.

2. Ultrarunning is a community.

As cheesy as it sounds, we are a family. That's why for Shacky and I, it's important to attend races even when we're not running.

This is where volunteering, trail work, cheering, crewing, and pacing play an important role. There's always work to be done at an ultra, and there are always runners who could use some motivation.

It doesn't matter if it's not your race. It's somebody's race. So you show up for them. You show up for the race directors who have too much to do. You show up for the volunteers who are tired, cold, and sleep-deprived. You show up for your friends who are running. For the runner whose pacer didn't show. For the newbie without a crew. You just show up.

Although Shacky and I love to joke about sitting around drinking beer at ultras (and there's a lot of that too), it's equally important to me that we jump when there's work to be done. I was proud at one race when Shacky had to drop out at an aid station, and ended up hanging out there to volunteer, pack up the aid station, and lift all the heavy objects because he noticed the volunteers were all older than he was.

When I think about this sport, I imagine the passing of a baton. So many of these older guys have put in their time. They have forged the trails for us (sometimes literally). They have put in the hours of trail work, the volunteer time, and have set a humble example for us. Now we are the ones who are young, able, and on fresh legs. It's time to get our hands dirty and make these events happen.

3. It's not really about the running.

I can agree that the running itself is pretty unimpressive and pointless. But it was never really about the running. It's about the way a runner feels when they finish their first ultra. It's about that realization when you cross the finish line at a 100-miler, that you actually are capable of anything you set your mind to.

It's that sense of accomplishment, self-worth, and empowerment that spills over into every other aspect of your life. It makes you hold your head up higher, gives you courage to shed those toxic relationships, inspires you in your career, helps you raise your family better, and motivates you to live healthfully and happily. That's why I run ultras, and why I encourage others to do so.

The physical act of covering random mileage is indeed senseless. But knowing for a fact that your body and mind are capable of far more than you thought— that is life changing.

4. You're not as awesome as you think you are.

The runners with the most experience tend to be the most humble. That's because they know that no matter what, there's always someone who is faster. Someone who has run further, or who is injured less.

With ultrarunning, you never know who you're talking to, so never brag about yourself. For all you know, the person you're talking to runs your weekly mileage in one day. Or she could be a world record-holder. You can never tell by looking at her. So avoid looking like an idiot, and shut your mouth.

So what's the verdict? Are we all just a bunch of attention whores? Perhaps some would argue we are. But in my experience, there is just as much opportunity to be giving, humble, and truly make a difference in someone else's life.

On My First Mountain 100

Chimera 100 was the first race I registered for that I truly believed I could not finish. Described one of the hardest mountain 100s in California, this event has inspired its fair share of horror stories.

The Chimera of Greek mythology is a ferocious, fire-breathing beast made up of part lion, part serpent, and part goat. She is a terror, but also swift-footed and strong. She sprints the mountain trails of this course, devouring runners and claiming her victims one DNF (Did Not Finish) at a time. On this race of incessant climbs and quad-shredding descents, you have only two choices:

Fall prey to the Beast. Or run at her side.

I knew Chimera was out of my league, but I also knew that if I trained hard I had a chance of finishing. And if I didn't, at least I challenged myself and hopefully learned something.

For a few weeks, I approached Chimera with a "race that I will try" mentality. But the Beast smells fear from miles away, so I knew I had to change my mindset. I adopted a new approach:

- Do or do not. There is no try.
- You don't have to be fast, but you better be fearless.
- Are you a Mexi-CAN or a Mexi-CAN'T??!

I would finish this race no matter how bloodied or broken. Quitting was not an option. This is the story of how I survived.

When I ran Javelina 100, I overheard a runner encourage another by saying, "It's only one 50K in the morning, one in the afternoon, one at night, and then a short 10-mile loop." That made sense to me, so for Chimera I broke down the race into three parts:

- The first 50K I would run as the Serpent.
- For the next 50K I would be the Goat.
- And in the final push I would be Lion.

1. Serpent

The serpent is one of the oldest symbols in mythology. One of the first things I ever learned was the Biblical story of Adam and Eve falling prey to the crafty serpent. The serpent is shrewd and cunning. And that's what I need to be early in this race.

Strategy in a 100-miler is everything. The key is to hold back as much as possible and preserve your body. I did this by keeping my body loose, slowing down, and not bombing any downhills. I made sure I never felt like I was exerting myself or breathing heavily. In fact, the first time I actually pushed myself to run was at mile 70+, when the sun came out on Sunday morning.

I love downhill running on single track, so I really had to make an effort to slow down and not fly these sections. I knew that I would need my quads later on. Tons of people passed me early in the race, and on every out and back section I noticed there were less and less people behind me. I was in the back of the pack.

2. Goat

Before I left for Chimera, I posted on my Facebook status: "How can a goat be afraid of the mountain? It is his home." That's how I felt going into this race. I had no jitters—just excitement. I had never run this far in the mountains before, but I knew I belonged in the clouds.

As Sarah Duffy points out on the Chimera Facebook page: "The course description includes 16 different terms for UP." Some include:

- Steep Up
- VERY Up
- Decomposed Granite Up
- Truck Trail Up
- Uphill Danger
- Rolling Up
- Generally Good Footing Uphill

There are also 15 different terms for DOWN:

- Steep Technical Down
- DANGER Down
- Rolling Down
- Very Rocky Downhill
- Short Rocky Down
- Slight Down Rocky

Sarah continues: "It was a purely physical challenge. I finished a climb and there was another one. I got to the bottom and I had to turn around and go back up. I rounded the bend and the hill continued on. I am still overwhelmed by the sheer physical demand of all that climbing, but I'll recover happily knowing the monstrous fire-breathing creature didn't eat me alive."

Fabrice Hardel won Chimera two years in a row and currently holds the course record (he broke his own record from the previous year) with a mind-blowing time of 16:52:06. After Cuyamaca 100K, Fabrice gave me the following advice for Chimera: Find the steepest hill you can and run up and down, over and over again.

He was dead on.

I channeled my inner goat and embraced the climbs. Rather than seeing them as something outside of me that I must conquer, I imagined myself playing in my own living room. The hills were neither strange nor foreign. They were a part of who I was. They were hard, relentless, and beautiful. Just like me. I tried to remember that I wanted to be here. Even if there were no race, no buckle, no accolades, I would still want to run.

Positivity was crucial. This I learned at Javelina, and made sure my mind was clear and motivated the entire distance. To me this means not allowing myself to get caught up in the stress of the race. I don't allow myself to think of the cutoffs. I don't wear a watch so I can't stress over my pace, and I eat consistently. When I'm having a dip, I stop and mentally address it.

Something like this:

- I'm feeling grouchy right now because I haven't eaten enough. I will stop to eat at the next aid station.

- I'm feeling worried right now because I don't think I will make the cutoff. I have plenty of time.

Stress can lead to physical pain if I don't put a stop to it. It's a wave of desperation and exhaustion that hits all at once and makes everything suck. With every race I do, I'm learning to control it more and more.

3. Lion

Having "preserved my body" for the first 60 miles, it was now time for beast mode. I pulled into an aid station about 30 minutes before sunrise, and was informed of a new danger:

"Do you have a pacer?" a volunteer asked.

"No."

"We recommend that people run with pacers, because there is a mountain lion from here to the next aid station."

"Oh. Ok...."

I still didn't have a pacer.

I remembered my mountain lion encounter at the Grand Canyon and decided it would be best to avoid this new obstacle. I tried shining my light into the bushes where the lion might be hiding, but that was useless. My light was only strong enough to illuminate my next few steps.

Instead, I decided to sing loudly. Surely my terrible singing voice would terrify the lion and send him fleeing into the mountains. That must have worked because the sun came up and I never saw any other lion besides myself.

As soon as the sun rose, I started running. I ran into the Indian Truck Trail aid station, and was greeted warmly. The volunteers were so eager to help and I got star treatment. I also had a cup of the most delicious homemade butternut squash soup with avocado. Refueled, I ran the seven miles down Indian Truck Trail to meet my pacer Holly.

At the bottom of the trail, I changed my socks, got into some dry clothes, re-taped my foot (preventative), and grabbed some gaiters (sleeves that protect pebbles from entering your shoes). It was such a relief to see Shacky again. The last time I had seen him was at mile 20, after the first single track loop—the day before.

Even Ginger and Momma Cat came out to say hello. Ginger licked all the salt off my face while Kitty loudly demanded to know why she had not been recently petted. I gave her a quick pet, but I couldn't stay long—we still had a lot of climbing left. I started hiking back up the hill with Holly.

It has been said of Chimera that "even the downhills feel like uphills," and that is certainly true in the last 10 miles especially. As soon as you hit a downhill stretch, you realize that you have no quads left. Thankfully, I had worked so hard to preserve mine that I had some leeway to run or at least walk comfortably downhill.

I was in such high spirits chatting with Holly. The mountains were beautiful, we were moving through the clouds, and Shacky had packed me a large ziplock bag full of watermelon, apples, avocado, and grapes.

We also picked up some clementines at the next aid station. I almost ate the entire fruit bag.

It's impossible for me to be sad on a mountain. I've been in San Diego for more than a year now, but I still feel like a tourist when I run at these spectacular elevations. It never gets old.

The downhill stretches were tricky because they were so steep that it was harder to walk them than to run. But running this late in the race is hard to do as well. There were no comfortable options.

I had to remember that the Lion doesn't represent comfort. It represents strength and power. And with the blessing of the Chimera She-Beast, I ran it in. As sick as it sounds, I was almost sad to see it end. I was having such a great time with Holly and I knew that stopping would be more uncomfortable than running at this point.

I finished in 31:52:31. I didn't realize it at the time, but finishers who complete the course under 30 hours get a silver buckle. I'll be back another year to claim my silver buckle and play in the mountains with my old friend Chimera.

Yes, she is as vicious as they say. She haunts these mountains because she can be herself here: crafty, fearless, and strong. She does share her trails, but only with other beasts.

On Retirement

Last May, I sat in the lobby of my office building waiting for Shacky to pick me up. It was the Thursday before Memorial Day and many of my co-workers were excited about the long weekend. One guy seemed especially excited. As he left, he told me, "I took Friday off as well, so I get an extra long weekend! I can't wait for the time off!"

I was excited too, but for a very different reason. I knew that as soon as I left that building, I would never again work a single day of my life.

I was 29 years old.

Since that day, I have often pondered the definition of "work." Technically speaking, we all work whether we get paid for it or not. We clean our houses. We raise our kids. We train for races. We go to our jobs. All of the above is work in the sense that it takes effort and energy.

But when I quit my job, my definition of never working again was simple: I will never again do anything for pay that I wouldn't be happy to do for free.

For many, that rules out most aspects of our jobs, and that was the case for me.

I did like some aspects of my job as an editor. I loved reading and writing and researching. When I went home in the evenings, I would do more of these activities for free. So these are all things I still do.

Running is another thing that I do for free and also love. Some of my races are sponsored, and some are not. Regardless of whether or not I am sponsored, I will still run. It doesn't feel like work.

The question then becomes, how do we live without an income? For my boyfriend and I, the answer was a tremendous downsize. When we both left our jobs, we moved into a small Rialta RV, and began traveling the country to run. I started writing this book.

Today, we happily have everything we need on only $15,000/year. We have unlimited freedom, and are rich in experiences. Our society has set us up to believe that money is the only reasonable way to acquire what we want or need. Nothing could be further from the truth.

To date, we have received thousands of dollars in goods and services without spending a dime. Rather than paying money, we pay by exchanging other goods or services: trading or bartering or writing reviews.

For example, I can help promote a product in exchange for free swag or a sponsored race entry. Because I am not making a huge profit, I am adamant about only promoting products that I truly believe are great, ones I use on a regular basis.

Between slashing our expenses and negotiating exchanges and trades, Shacky and I survive on surprisingly little each month. The money I make on the side through writing helps keep us afloat. Any additional profits allow us to sponsor other runners for races they cannot afford on their own.

Our existence is simple and understated. We value freedom, self-sufficiency, and not much else. We long to enjoy life while we are young, healthy, and full of energy. Fame and riches hold no appeal for us.

The trade-off is that:

- I will never be rich. The more I make, the more I will give away.
- I will never have a home to decorate. The trails and mountains will be my home.
- I will never have a long-term plan. I will live day-by-day and pursue my whims as they come.
- I will never have a bucket list. Because why wait? We'll make it a "To Do" list.
- I will never work another day in my life.

Writing this book was the first thing I did after quitting my job. As of today, we have traveled across eight glorious states, and I have seen such beauty all over this country. I am learning so much about who I am, what I love, and where I belong.

This is what I am meant to be doing. And my adventure has only just begun.

Vanessa Runs

Acknowledgements

Robert Shackelford

My boyfriend Shacky is the anchor without which none of this would have been possible. Not this book, not the RV, not this lifestyle. Shacky took a chance on me when he barely knew who I was, and I can hardly believe how well it has worked out. I have some pretty crazy ideas that would scare most men, but Shacky just nods his head and says it's doable. He's my best friend and trail buddy and I have no interest in imagining a life without him.

Ginger Shackelford and Momma Shackelford

Our furry children are "only" animals (dog and cat), but so much a part of our family that I have to include them. They teach me what life is really about — bounding with joy through the mountains, and then promptly passing out hours later in exhaustion. Or just being lazy all day. They don't taper. They don't contain their excitement. They live every moment genuinely and never hide their true personalities. They have taught me so much.

Ulises Rodriguez and Angela Rodriguez

Although the parents who raised me were human and imperfect like the rest of us, they never once failed in their support of my writing. They believed in me wholeheartedly, and me writing a book was my dad's dream as well as my own. It was obvious to them that this was my talent, and they encouraged me as much as they could. I have much to thank them for.

Eli, Emma, Kayla, Natalie Rodriguez

My sisters are awesome and so important in helping me become the person I am today. I have so many joyful memories with them, and anyone who has a sister can understand how irreplaceable they are. I hope I have set a courageous example for them, so they can follow their own dreams boldly.

Ron, Barbara & Alison Covert

My step-grandparents and step-aunt were part of my life since I was 13, and were my first glimpse into a family so different than my own. They have supported my writing for years, offering me wise words of encouragement and advice.

Sonja Melconian

Every writer has that one teacher who inspired them deeply from a young age. For me, that was Ms. Melconian. I was a strange, sheltered kid when she met me, yet she wisely steered me in the right direction and was infinitely supportive of my talents. I am sorry to have lost touch with her, but trust she continues to inspire future writers.

Susan Fish at storywell.ca

My editor Susan has been a close family friend for years, and the first "real live" writer I ever met. I always admired her kindness and writing talent, and I am honored to have her help me on this book. Her edits have made all the difference.

The Ultra Community of Southern California

There are way too many people here to mention by name, but every single person embraced me into the ultra community when I moved to San Diego. I instantly had a new family. I am forever indebted to these amazing people, most of whom are much stronger runners than myself. They inspire me daily.

Interested in publishing your own book?

Ray Charbonneau can help you design and publish your book quickly, professionally, and at a low cost. Unlike other services that automate the process, Ray will work directly with you every step of the way to ensure you get the book you want.

For more information, visit the Y42K Book Production Services page at:

http://www.y42k.com/bookproduction.html

Made in the USA
Charleston, SC
02 April 2013